Hunting and Fishing in the Great Smokies

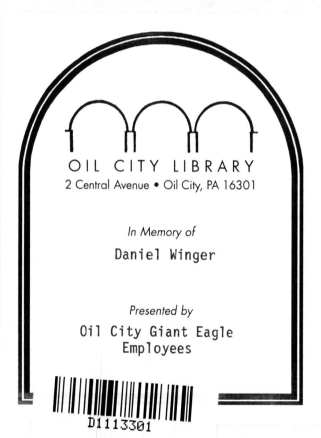

OIL CITY LIBRARY
2 Central Avenue • Oil City, PA 16301

In Memory of
Daniel Winger

Presented by
Oil City Giant Eagle
Employees

D1113301

Frontispiece from the original 1948 Knopf edition.

HUNTING AND FISHING IN THE GREAT SMOKIES

The Classic Guide for Sportsmen

Jim Gasque

WITH A NEW INTRODUCTION
BY JIM CASADA

The University of North Carolina Press
Chapel Hill

This book was published with the assistance of the Anniversary Endowment Fund of the University of North Carolina Press.

Originally published in 1948 by Alfred A. Knopf

Introduction to the paperback edition
© *2008 The University of North Carolina Press*

۔۔ۯ

A portion of the proceeds of the sale of this book is being
donated to Trout Unlimited's Embrace-A-Stream program to
protect, reconnect, restore, and sustain coldwater fisheries in
the Great Smoky Mountains National Park.

۔۔ۯ

The paper in this book meets the guidelines for permanence
and durability of the Committee on Production Guidelines for
Book Longevity of the Council on Library Resources.

The University of North Carolina Press has been a member
of the Green Press Initiative since 2003.

Complete cataloging data for this book is available
from the Library of Congress.

ISBN 978-0-8078-5915-5

12 11 10 09 08   5 4 3 2 1

University of North Carolina Press books may be purchased at a discount
for educational, business, or sales promotional use. For information,
please visit www.uncpress.unc.edu or write to UNC Press, attention: Sales
Department, 116 South Boundary Street, Chapel Hill, NC 27514-3808.

To
Captain R. D. Gatewood

Contents

Introduction to the Paperback Edition   xi

Introduction   xxi

PART I. *Trout Streams and Trout Fishing in the Great Smokies*

   I. Cataloochee Creek   3

  II. Deep Creek   10

 III. Hazel Creek   20

 IV. Other Smoky Streams   28

  V. Little Streams   34

 VI. Mark Cathey   41

VII. Other Trout Streams   55

VIII. Smallmouth Streams   63

PART II. *Lake Fishing in the Great Smokies*

  IX. Fontana   75

   X. Nantahala   85

  XI. Chatuge   91

 XII. Hiwassee   100

XIII. Santeetlah   107

XIV. Other Lakes   118

 XV. Tackle   129

XVI. Rules and Regulations   133

CONTENTS

PART III. *Hunting in the Great Smokies*

	Author's Note	139
XVII.	Bear: Distinguished Hunters—Famous Bears	141
XVIII.	The Black Bear: Habits and Characteristics	147
XIX.	Bear: Ranges—Season—Guides—Division	153
XX.	The Russian Boar: American History—Characteristics	157
XXI.	Hunting the Boar	169
XXII.	Boar: Localities—Regulations—Guides	176
XXIII.	The Plott Hounds	180
XXIV.	Deer	185
XXV.	Grouse	192
XXVI.	Squirrels to Order	200
XXVII.	Fontana Village	205
	Conclusion	209
	Index	211

Illustrations

Facing page

Frontispiece from the original edition   iii

Dr. Kelly Bennett fishes at Indian Creek Falls, ca. 1940   xi

Carl Grueninger Jr. with his first rainbow trout, 1939 or 1940   32

R. Q. Woody Sr. on a bridge over Noland Creek, 1941   33

Mark Cathey, near Deep Creek, 1944   48

The grave of Mark Cathey in the Bryson City Cemetery   49

Dr. Kelly Bennett rides a boat on Fontana Lake, ca. 1945   80

The old I. K. Stearns place, known as Solola Lodge   81

Swain County hunters and their bear dogs, ca. 1920s   144

Swain County bear hunters, ca. 1920s   145

Dr. Kelly Bennett of Bryson City—a great apostle of the Smokies and a promoter of the Blue Ridge Parkway, the creation of the Great Smoky Mountains National Park, the Cherokee Historical Association, and tourism in western North Carolina—fishes for trout at the foot of Indian Creek Falls, ca. 1940. The pool was located on land owned by famed angler Mark Cathey prior to creation of the park in 1934. (Image courtesy of Jim Casada)

Introduction to the Paperback Edition

Thanks to a variety of factors, the book reprinted here has held me in thrall since adolescence. Like me, its author, Jim Gasque, harbored a deep, abiding passion for our shared highland homeland in the Great Smokies of North Carolina. He devotes more space to Deep Creek, where I caught my first trout on a fly at the age of nine and became hopelessly hooked for life, than to any other stream covered in the work. Deep Creek and one of its principal feeders, Indian Creek, formed my "home water" as a boy, and so they have remained in all the marvelously misspent hours of angling since that time.

Until creation of the Great Smoky Mountains National Park in 1934, Indian Creek was home to legendary mountain sportsman Mark Cathey, a man Gasque so admired that he devotes an entire chapter to this delightfully eccentric character who epitomized the descriptive mountain word "quair." I never knew Cathey, who died just two years after my birth, but from my earliest fishing days, stories of his angling exploits provided by my father and a host of other boyhood fly-fishing heroes enchanted me. A trout from the Cathey Hole, situated on a stretch of Indian Creek where "Uncle Mark" owned property, was part of the first limit I ever creeled. Wading in Cathey's footsteps through the waters he had known and fished so well always stirred my soul. It is equally enjoyable to join him vicariously, through Jim Gasque's words, in a sporting world of yesteryear.

Those intensely personal considerations of place and people factored prominently in this book's early appeal for me, but that's only part of the story. Beginning somewhere in the mid-1950s, less than a decade after *Hunting and Fishing in the Great Smokies* was published, I checked the work out from the Marianna Black Library in my little hometown of Bryson City at least twice a year—once as spring and the opening of trout season approached and again in the early fall when hunting lay just around the corner.

Those carefree days of youth have long since come and gone, but a sense of linkage to Gasque and his book remains as strong as ever. It still forms an especially worthy companion for a session of armchair adventure, and delving through its pages invariably warms my heart as I am carried gladly back to countless days of tight lines and fine times. Such sentiments are not, however, merely those of an incurable romantic with a yen to look back that strengthens with the passage of each year.

Others share my perspective, as I am reminded annually when The Fly Fishing Show is held in Charlotte, North Carolina. Over the years I've become pretty much a mainstay at the event as a seminar speaker, sharing my experiences on streams of the Smokies, harkening back to the days of characters such as Mark Cathey, and discussing tactics and techniques for catching trout in the high country.

As part of my arrangement with the show's promoters, I have a booth offering my own books as well as a selection of out-of-print titles with regional themes or an outdoor focus. Without fail, every year a handful of folks enamored of forgotten tales and long-lost trails will stop and ask me about the possibility of locating a copy of the present work. My stock usually includes a copy or two, since I've made a practice of perusing out-of-print booksellers' offerings for decades, but invariably there's a bit of sticker shock linked to the price when I quote it. That's thanks to the fact that, in the six plus decades since its publication, *Hunting and Fishing in the Great Smokies* has become quite difficult to locate, and those who own copies, especially if they are sportsmen or have direct connection with the mountains, treasure the book for the literary jewel it is.

⚜

We'll return to the book's nature and origins momentarily, but first it seems appropriate to share a bit more insight into the man who was Jim Gasque. In comparison with most of the other contributors to the Borzoi Books for Sportsmen series, of which the book was a part, Gasque (the name, pronounced *gas-kwee*, is of French Huguenot origin) is little known. Accounts of his early years are somewhat at variance. One suggests he was born near the North Carolina village of Morven (in Anson County) on March 30, 1903, and that his family moved to South Carolina when he was just a toddler. Another has him being born near Lake City, South Carolina. Whichever was the case, he was introduced to hunting and fishing at an early age by his father, McRoy Gasque, with whom he regularly enjoyed sporting outings in the Palmetto State during the younger Gasque's adolescent years.

In a slender, privately published volume entitled *Reminiscences*, Myrtle Lane Gasque (probably a sister, but this is not totally clear), shares a story little "Jimmie" wrote as a boy that gives an early hint of literary inclinations. She then notes that "fishing was his real obsession" and that warm months would find him "red from sunburn, fighting gnats and mosquitoes, fishing for minnows. Now and then he would catch one—Oh! The sublimity of such an hour—the thrill."

She likens him to Tom Sawyer, writes of how little girls thought him "an angel of a boy" even as he studiously ignored them, and speaks of how fishing was for him a "serious, breath-taking, soul-absorbing business." Then we are jerked rather rudely from those hal-cyon days of Jimmie's youth to the mid-1950s. "Time," she writes, "has a way of slipping by and with the passing of the years Jimmie has grown to manhood, and now, with the very latest and most approved methods, including some of his own inventions, he has from long experience and research in the art of angling become an outstanding authority in this favorite of outdoor sports, fishing."

Gasque's development as "an outstanding authority" came in western North Carolina. In 1919, his family moved to Asheville, the region's largest city, and that locale would be Jim's home for the rest of his life. It was there that he met, and in 1929 married, Viola Helen Bell. Both prior to and in the early years of his marriage Gasque pursued first one and then another career path in a manner that suggests the rootless, footloose nature of a man seeking his life's anchor. Among his positions was work as a diamond salesman and participation in the bail bonding business with his uncle, Jim Stikeleather (who figures prominently in the chapter on Hazel Creek in this book). Then, in 1936, he became co-owner of the Asheville Exterminating Company. With its flexibility in terms of work hours and its somewhat seasonal nature, the business suited Gasque perfectly. It left him ample time to fish, and he began supplementing his income by serving as a guide to visitors of the type his good friend Mark Cathey called "Yankee sports."

Gasque's fishing and hunting interests also led to another line of work, freelance writing. For many years, beginning in the mid-1930s, he wrote outdoor columns for both the *Asheville Citizen* and the *Asheville Times*, and he became a frequent contributor to national magazines such as *Field and Stream* and the sporting encyclopedias of the era. In time his skills and savvy as a guide led to creation of the Western North Carolina Sportsman's Service, and those who knew him hailed Gasque as the "wizard fisherman."

That wizardry certainly extended to his technical ability as an angler, because he taught fly-fishing, won numerous fly-casting competitions, and regularly gave casting demonstrations. Similarly, he was a gifted marksman who was equally adroit as a wingshooter and rifleman.

Gasque's fine coordination, as is exemplified by his expertise with the tools of the sportsman's trade, was nicely balanced by his efforts as a craftsman and inventor. He built high-dollar custom bamboo fly rods, tied his own trout flies as well as producing them commercially for Abercrombie & Fitch in New York, and invented several bass lures. These included the Gasque Crawler, Popstriker, and Basstriker. Local and family legend suggests that he coined the term "Whopper Stopper" and then later sold the rights to this famed bass plug.

Clearly a man of ample energy, Gasque also collected coins, participated in civic and political affairs, had an avid interest in North Carolina history, and was a keen gardener. He had a greenhouse where he grew vegetables throughout the year, and his horticultural experimentation led to the development of a variety of tomato known as Gasque's Pride. He was generous to a fault, and it was said that at his death "half the churches in Asheville owed him money" for his exterminating services. Gasque died on October 30, 1967. His wife survived him by many years, passing away in 1991. The couple, who had no children, is buried in the Avery's Creek United Methodist Church Cemetery in Arden, North Carolina.

⁂

Hunting and Fishing in the Great Smokies was a book in the famed Borzoi Books for Sportsmen series published by Alfred A. Knopf. With their sumptuous silk binding in deep burgundy; gilt title, author's name, and publisher's name adorning the spine; embossed

Borzoi dog logo on the front; and top-quality paper these books' packaging was as aesthetically appealing as their contents were consistently interesting. The works in the series were published between 1943 and 1955, and altogether there were thirty-one titles. Ten of these were carryovers from Penn Publishing Company, and collectively the list of contributors to the series reads like a Who's Who of hunting and fishing literature from the mid-twentieth century. Among the stable of authors in the Borzoi Books for Sportsmen were such renowned sporting scribes as Ray Bergman, Russell Annabel, Van Campen Heilner, and Jack O'Connor.

The scion of the publishing house that produced these books, Alfred A. Knopf, was in no sense a sportsman. He was a shrewd New York businessman with a flair for unusual attire (he regularly wore hot pink or bright green shirts with shoes and ties to match) and a keen eye for quality books. His idea, and it was a practical one, was to capitalize on the growing emergence of the American middle class, an upsurge in interest in sport spawned at least in part by World War II, and the rapid rise in automobile ownership by offering outdoor-related books that appealed to an affluent audience willing to spend money on hunting and fishing. According to M. L. "Duke" Biscotti, the author of *The Borzoi Books for Sportsmen*, an essential reference work for any serious student of the subject, Knopf was somewhat disappointed in the performance of the series. From the perspective of posterity, though, it produced some of the most important outdoor literature of the twentieth century.

Certainly Knopf would have been disappointed with the sales performance of *Hunting and Fishing in the Great Smokies*. The book, which was copyrighted in 1948, appeared in only a single edition. It was published simultaneously in Canada by the Ryerson Press. According to Knopf's sales and royalty records, the work, which was priced at $3.75, sold only 2,644 copies. It went out of print in 1956.

Given the comparative remoteness of the Smokies at the time, not to mention the fact that the coverage of hunting belonged strictly to history as far as the Great Smoky Mountains National Park was concerned (no hunting is allowed in national parks), this should come as no surprise. Then, as now, it was a work of the fireside or armchair adventure genre. As Duke Biscotti notes in his comments on the work in *The Borzoi Books for Sportsmen*, "It gives the Great Smoky mountains an almost mystical aura by Mr. Gasque's descriptions of unspoiled mountain trout streams and uninterrupted stretches of wilderness. His stories in this work depicting delightfully individualistic mountain men add to this mystique."

It seems possible that Knopf's decision to publish the book may have been predicated, at least in part, on the success of an earlier work of Gasque's. This was a straightforward "how to" treatment, *Bass Fishing*, which originally appeared in 1946, went through three printings, sold far better than the current work, and remained in print until 1962.

Viewed from any perspective, Jim Gasque's *Hunting and Fishing in the Great Smokies* ranks as a regional classic. Written in the simple, sprightly style of a gifted storyteller, the book carries the reader to streams of dreams and lakes of wonder. While most of the chapter titles suggest detailed coverage of a given creek, reservoir, or type of hunting, the chapters actually serve as a medium for the telling of tales set in a particular place or focused on a given game animal. For example, the treatment of Deep Creek is almost entirely devoted to recollections of memorable moments Gasque experienced there, and much the same holds true for storied Hazel Creek and the Oconaluftee River (which he spells "Oconalufty").

Two chapters in the work deserve special comment. The one dealing with Mark Cathey, perhaps the most famous of all high country outdoorsmen, is Gasque at his best. He personally knew

Uncle Mark, as Cathey was fondly known in his later years, and shared his company on fishing trips. Cathey was a woodsman par excellence, and his "dance of the dry fly," using his favorite pattern, a Grey hackle Yellow, earned him plaudits long before northeastern writers began to suggest fishing the dry fly as a living insect. A lifelong bachelor with quaint mountain ways and an irresistible personality, Cathey captivated Gasque in much the same fashion he delighted all who knew him well.

Local old-timers still love to regale eager audiences with stories of Cathey and his exploits, and certainly Gasque did his part to preserve for posterity the lore surrounding the man and his milieu. Strangely, though, he does not mention the epitaph of Cathey's tombstone, which rests within casting distance of the massive boulder marking the grave of another mountain legend, Horace Kephart. Written by Reverend W. Herbert Brown, a fisherman and friend of Cathey, it is, in my studied opinion, as appropriate an inscription as one could possibly ask for. It reads: "Mark Cathey, beloved hunter and fisherman, was himself caught by the Gospel hook just before the season closed for good."

Another chapter of special note is that dealing with the Plott hound. A hunting dog for the ages, which traces its roots to the time when the Plott family settled in Haywood County, North Carolina, in the eighteenth century, the breed has long been a favorite among mountain bear hunters. Gasque does it full justice, as is equally true of his coverage of fabled bear hunters such as Big Tom Wilson and Mark Cathey.

Difficult to obtain in the original version, and pricey to boot, the book might well have been reprinted before now. It does for the outdoor scene in the Smokies of bygone days what works such as Margaret W. Morley's *The Carolina Mountains*, Robert L. Mason's *The Lure of the Great Smokies*, Horace Kephart's *Our Southern High-*

landers, and Olive Tilford Dargan's *From My Highest Hill* do for mountain folkways. Certainly for anyone desirous of taking flights of fancy into the fields and forests of the North Carolina mountains as they once were, for those interested in developing an understanding of just how prominently hunting and fishing figure in the culture of the high country, or for anyone simply interested in a "good read," this is a regional classic promising a full measure of armchair pleasure. As you read it, pause and ponder the scenes Gasque describes, and as you do so perhaps offer silent thanks for the existence of the Great Smoky Mountains National Park and the Nantahala and Pisgah National Forests. In these vast expanses of public land it is still possible to enjoy precisely the type of sports that Gasque so enjoyed and which he described with vivid accuracy—and somehow one likes to think that the old "wizard fisherman" would be pleased by that fact.

Introduction

In treating the fish and game life of the Great Smoky region, there is no better way to give a perspective of the whole range than to review briefly that portion of it known as the Great Smoky Mountains National Park, because the forest and wild life is much the same over the entire range. Situated astride the North Carolina–Tennessee border and lying almost equally in the two states, the Great Smokies proper are the greatest mountain mass east of the Rockies. De Soto is said to have visited the mountains, but as late as a few decades ago they were little known to the outside world. The Great Smoky Mountains National Park, authorized by Act of Congress in 1926 and comprising 440,000 acres of the Smoky Range, is a wilderness of mountains that for seven hundred square miles of area lift their lovely peaks 5,000 feet into the air, sixteen of them reaching more than 6,000 feet. Frontier conditions, long since vanished elsewhere, still exist here, where communities remain intact, typical of the crude, self-sufficient life, traditional and characteristic of the region for generations. Many of the present white population are descendants of the early settlers, who were colonists from England and Scotland. They have lived for centuries largely to themselves, in seclusion from the outside world.

These mountains are also the home of the Cherokee Indians, whose descendants now live on the Qualla Indian Reservation, situated on the southern fringe of the range and skirted by the beautiful Oconalufty River. It would perhaps be more accurate to say that the present Indians descend from those few who escaped to the mountain fastness when the rest of the tribe was removed to Oklahoma in 1838.

In the Smoky area some fifty species of fur-bearing animals, two hundred birds, sixty fishes, thirty-four reptiles, and more than thirty amphibians have been found. An angler reading about the fish life of the Great Smokies, or anticipating a visit with rod and reel to their hundreds of miles of trout and bass waters, would be interested in its virgin forests and vegetation, more numerous and varied than that of any other range in America, since the character of this forest and vegetation is closely related to and is the principal factor controlling the nature, quality, and clarity of its streams.

The most extensive forest of virgin red spruce in the United States and hardwoods that have never been spoiled by the woodsman's ax are to be found here. More than one hundred and twenty-five species of native trees and eighteen other varieties, not native, have been identified. Red spruces, hemlocks, chestnuts, yellow birches, red maples, tulip poplars, black cherries, buckeyes, silverbells—all become giant specimens of their kind.

Of its wide varieties of plant life, many, regarded as shrubs elsewhere, thrive and become arborescent in the rich mountain soil. Specimens of mountain laurel exceeding seventy inches at the base, with limbs in proportion, occur. Ivy and rhododendron also grow to great size. No area in North America contains a corresponding plant life. Twelve hundred flowering plants, almost as many fungi, three hundred mosses, two hundred lichens, and one hundred liverworts have been found. The earlier flowers in the lowlands appear near the end of January, while the latest frequently hold their blossoms into December. April and May find many spring flowers at their peak, such as dogwood and the abundant mountain laurel. Flame azalea and pink rhododendron are usually at their best during the month of July. The height of coloration comes in autumn, the foliage making its greatest display throughout the usually sunny month of October.

Late spring and early summer days are seasonably warm, but in higher altitudes even midsummer days are pleasantly cool, with the nights becoming chilly. In late summer and early autumn, when the rainfall is lowest, weather conditions are usually ideal. Snow and rain occur during the winter, but all transmountain and intersecting highways are normally accessible.

Aside from the transmountain highway from Bryson City, North Carolina, via Cherokee Indian Reservation to Gatlinburg, Tennessee, and many secondary roads, there are more than seven hundred miles of trails—many of them typical streamside trails, trodden by fishermen for decades.

In the Smoky Range proper there are seven hundred miles of trout and smallmouth bass streams. The most noted of the thirty-odd trout streams are Cataloochee Creek, Oconalufty River, Deep Creek, the famous Hazel Creek (visited by many on this continent), Abrams Creek, Little River proper and its prongs, and the prongs of Little Pigeon River. Particularly inviting to the dry-fly man, these streams, flowing through beautiful valleys of lush green vegetation in the lower park areas, and the upper waters sloped by great ranges of cliffs, bluffs, and ridges, *rarely* become soiled. The rainfall not absorbed by the rich black earth drains easily and lightly over the leaves and mosses into the streams, thus creating a region of crystal-clear waters.

Rainbow trout, native brook trout, and smallmouth bass take precedence within the park boundaries, but the streams and lakes of the surrounding country offer an even wider variety. Aside from the many streams of the Smokies, there are several other near-by mountain ranges that have more than a hundred trout streams and similar forest and plant life.

Spreading over a large belt of the southern Appalachians, some of the best fishing lakes in the South offer an abundance of game fish such as the largemouth and smallmouth bass, the rainbow trout, walleyed pike, muskellunge, sauger, and several of the better pan fishes. The streams and lakes overlapping from western North Carolina into the adjoining states and covering a three-hundred-mile strip of the country and almost half that in breadth, are treated just as I've known and found them for more than a score of years.

Since the days of Daniel Boone the southern Appalachians have been a great hunting region. Among big-game hunters the black bear, the deer and the Russian boar take precedence, the bear and deer inhabiting more than a two-hundred-mile series of connecting mountain ranges, the boar occupying a more limited area near the Great Smokies. For a long number of seasons their abundance has remained and continues sufficient to attract hunters from many parts of the country.

Of our game birds, this part of the country is most noted for its ruffed grouse. This fine bird is plentiful almost wherever there are mountains. Gunning for them is one of the best of outdoor sports, and in this rugged country seems to have little effect on their numbers. There are also quail and other small game. Hunting in the Smoky region and the southern Appalachians is hunting in a country where there's game. Whether a hunter, following the trail of our Southeastern game, wants to collect a pelt or cut a few grouse feathers, the sincere aim of this book is to give a true picture of just the kind of hunting he will find.

A long-held and deep conviction that the extraordinary merits of our Great Smokies and the southern Appalachians are too little known and appreciated, a pleasant association for three decades with their lakes and streams, mountains and valleys, and the gentle persuasion of friends are responsible for the work between these covers, and have made it, indeed, a labor of love.

ᏺ PART ONE ᏺ

Trout Streams and
Trout Fishing in
the Great Smokies

CHAPTER I

Cataloochee Creek

The fly hovered for an instant, then settled lightly on the rim of an eddy. It had traveled but a few feet on its downstream journey when there was a flash of silver, a splash, and a gasping sigh from an angler—a sigh drowned instantly by the whine of the reel. Another Cataloochee rainbow made for the fast water.

No other opening could so well introduce this great stream. Rising in the higher Smokies, the Cataloochee stems from the junction of a few spring-fed trickles. Wandering northeast through virgin and semi-virgin forest, it gathers substance and power, and when it bursts from the park boundary into more open country, it has attained river status.

To anglers, it is one of the most fascinating streams in the Smokies, owing to its normally peaceful character and its hundreds of pools. The experienced fly fisherman has but to look at the "Cataloochee" (as the natives call it) to be impressed by its "trouty" appearance. The average angler is inclined to quicken his pace in fishing, for the vista of pools ahead have the "greener pasture" appeal, but not on Cataloochee.

As to what may be expected from the standpoint of creel weight, it will perhaps be of interest to go back twenty-five years and review briefly just how this stream, from that time to this, has treated both local and transient anglers.

In the early twenties, when better roads—or shall we say just roads?—began to make Cataloochee available to others than the native mountain pole fishers, this stream in a few years earned the reputation of being the stream of "big" trout. That was back in the days when fishermen of the region were becoming more dry-fly conscious and more "artificial"-minded. But it was still a day when worming and other bait methods were common practice as compared with the seldom applied fancier ways of taking trout. With the hackled frauds steadily replacing the can of worms, however, it is interesting how Cataloochee, was acclaimed almost overnight a great dry-fly stream.

It came about one bright mid-spring day when two anglers from the North arrived in Asheville. From all reports of that day they bore the reputation of being finished dry-fly men, anglers who in this finer art of deceiving had established their names among the fishermen of their time. They had come down to western Carolina by invitation to look over and fish some of the Smoky streams. The following day they were taken fishing by a local gentleman known to be a good "trouter." To sample our mountain waters with their fine leaders and flies, Cataloochee was selected as the most likely stream. Their host preferred to observe rather than fish, being curious to see what men of their caliber could do on a Southern stream. He was more than rewarded.

Fishing that first morning began in the lower waters. The patterns of dry flies used weren't recorded, but the size was. Favoring tens and twelves, tied to a longer tapered leader than customary in these parts, they started casting to the spacious pools that occur so frequently on this creek. Fishing along together, taking the pools alternately, here is what happened. Two fine fish, ranging in the higher teen inches, were taken from the first pool; as they went on upstream, two others were hooked and netted from the next two pools, both running well in the teens; and as they worked pool after pool that morning, it was one repeat performance after another with, in the course of events, a twenty-two-incher coming to net. Indeed, it was a fine beginning. But what I think makes this story worth relating was the highlight of the day, which came in the afternoon.

About the time they were thinking of calling it a day, they approached a series of three pools. The first was separated from the second by a fast run-off of about a hundred feet, while the upper pool was separated from the middle one by a shorter length of very fast water. At the lower pool nothing happened. But as the man who was to have his turn at the middle pool approached within casting-distance of its tail water, he stopped abruptly, then backtracked a couple of steps. There was a motion of his hand that had an unmistakable meaning. It was a motion to his companions cautioning them to approach very quietly to where he was standing. In a moment the three men were looking at a shape in the slow-moving water near the tail of the pool. The object that had their attention was loafing lazily in water about four feet deep. Presently, as something floated down that he wanted to inhale, he drifted to a point where his nose touched the surface, then settled to a lower depth again. He was about the size of a man's leg, but not as long of course, and the hooked jaw (very obvious even at that distance) indicated that he was a male. After a brief conference a coin was flipped to see who would cast to the monster. At first each insisted the other do so, but it seemed best to settle the matter by chance. They were looking at something that made three men a little shaky about the knees, something that without question was custodian of that pool—something whose survival through a long life could only be attributed to his ability to manage difficulties, including a few buggy things with gut attached, something that looked most formidable idling there in his aquatic pasture.

The first cast was made up and across by the hands of an expert who knew how to deposit both his fly and his leader in water of the same speed. With no least vestige of a "drag" the fly floated down right over his nose, but from a position of about two feet below surface he didn't move. Flawlessly a second cast was completed, and as it passed over this time he moved slowly to within a foot of the surface, but made no effort to take. When he held that near-surface position, all three men were trembling. A third time the fly was cast and started its lazy float downstream. When it was about four feet from his nose, the great tail moved, and a second later two objects met—very gracefully he sucked in the fly.

The instant the hook was set, he turned for deeper water. As the line tightened and the rod bent sharply, he made a rush to the upper end of the pool and then another swift run back down the pool, after which he turned again and began to circle the deeper water, but at a slower pace. This he continued until he had circled the pool several times. When a little more rod was applied to swing him closer in, he showed his stripes two feet above surface. In another instant he was digging at the bottom of the pool. There was no chance, for a while of Old Fighter being led into shallow water. When dislodged from the pool bottom, he made several dashes up and down the pool, then began to circle again. The constant rod pressure was now tiring him, and it looked as if the climax might come in this pool, but he wasn't through yet. On the last circle he was led in closer. At the sight of man he did the unexpected. In the space of a few seconds he had carried the fly, leader, line, and fisherman through the fast run of water to the pool above. It would have seemed more logical for him to have gone downstream, but it was soon evident why he went up. He had lived up there and remembered the log that lay deep in that pool; he would have a chance to do something with the bug that was stinging him in the nose. There he had twice before rubbed a bait fisher's hook out of his jaw. But after this mad dash up fast water, with the rod tip that had followed him growing constantly stronger, he had little opportunity to take advantage of the log. In fact, he was turned just before he got there. A few less healthy dashes below his log that he could never quite reach, and he began to weaken; his sense of direction grew less keen. As the play continued and the rod got stronger, he began to lean a little to one side—he felt very tired now. But presently he saw two legs and a net—and with a spurt of fresh life he was off downstream again.

When followed to the pool where all this started, he grew suddenly very quiet. Close observation revealed about six inches of tail sticking out from under a rock that shelved the shallow side of the pool. A gentle tugging went unnoticed, or at least it failed to move him. It was obvious he would be content to stay under that rock. For a long ten minutes he continued indifferent, refusing to budge. Finally he became rested, and with rest he became more conscious of stinging sensation. The bending and relaxing of a rod tip was doing its work. His nose was now getting very sore. Presently he began waving his tail just a little—another way of probable escape was now occurring to him. Suddenly he shot out from under the rock, headed downpool. He reasoned that this was far greater than all former emergencies, and he knew just where he was going. In two or three seconds he was on his way to the pool below. He had lived there too. Through the stretch of fast water he went like a little freight train coasting downgrade, with nothing but a fine 3X leader to brake a little and maintain the connection. Once in the pool below, he tried to hide under a big rock on the far side, so there would be a lot of deep water between him and his enemy. But this pool was his undoing—after a few brave tries up and down and crosswise, he hadn't the strength left to move out again. After a final skirmish near the depths of the pool he gave up suddenly, his exhaustion complete. In the net he was a magnificent specimen of his kind—to this day the largest ever reported taken from Cataloochee on a dry fly.

[7]

This experience, which happened nearly three decades ago, is how Cataloochee was introduced to the local anglers as a great dry-fly stream. But the angler should not let this story deceive him into expecting this brand of fishing; it was an uncommon occurrence, far surpassing the usual. Throughout a long span of years, however, this creek has come to be one of the Smokies' favorites. As with any stream, it has its off years, but on the whole it has consistently measured up to the angler's expectations. While the stream is most favored for the dry fly, it may be noted that the larger fish nowadays seem to be taken by the spinner and spinner-fly method.

As an example of this I'm reminded of two fishermen, both local men, who are among the best in the art of spinner fishing. For years they have been conspicuously associated with big trout, and their methods of bringing many of these to net are well known. They know well all the large pools on Cataloch, and when they go after "big 'uns" they use but one method. With each of them it is alike, and very simple at that; I know no way of using artificials that is more effective. A large fly—nothing smaller than a No. 4 or No. 6 (one of these men regularly uses a Royal Coachman)—is attached to a spinner, usually a No. 3, nothing smaller than a No. 2. They have little preference between the Idaho and Colorado shapes. Small lead shot are strung about a foot apart almost the full length of their leader, but so as to detract as little as possible from the natural action of the fly and spinner, the tail shot being never too close to the spinner, and the spinner left to revolve freely. With such a rig they fish the larger pools right down to the bottom, showing little preference as to fishing up or down or crosswise, for in thus working the big pools, rules and niceties give way to depth fishing. Precisely as revealed above, these men, year after year, have brought in many large trout, some of them ranging up to two feet. During the last ten to fifteen years this has been the most effective method by which the really big fish have been consistently taken from Cataloochee. On the other hand, the greater numbers of trout are taken on the dry fly.

As in most streams in more recent years, the creek census indicates that the annual take on this stream does not average as high as it did formerly. However, as may be proved on bright days by the use of polaroid glasses, big fish are still to be seen. They will not often take, and one wonders if with time the big ones aren't growing wiser to the angler's frauds. Anyway, from the time it was made accessible by better roads, Cataloochee has appealed to the higher level of the purists. It is a stream that any dry-fly man will delight to add to his list. It has held up remarkably well, and there are two reasons for this. Aside from adequate stocking, a recent stream survey of western North Carolina by a competent entomologist shows this creek to be surpassed by none in quantity of stream-bed food supply.

On higher Cataloochee there are several quaint tributaries. Caldwell Fork and Rough Fork are the ones of most interest. In these higher waters some brook trout are found along with the rainbow. When visiting this stream, one should go well shod. It has perhaps the most slippery bottom of any stream in the Smokies, but what a stream it is!

CHAPTER II

Deep Creek

An angler's thoughts on a stream are always colored by the sharp memory of one excursion to that stream. I can think of no better way of describing the delights of Deep Creek than by reliving four memorable days spent on its margins.

The afternoon before was spent casting to the rainbows of Forney Creek—a sort of preliminary warm-up to our long-planned trip to the upper waters of Deep Creek. Captain Gatewood and I, after a final checkup on our items of duffel, had retired. Before the light was turned out that night, a whipping rain had begun, and as it threshed the cabin roof I was apprehensive that our carefully laid plans might be doomed. The Captain, however, not to be discouraged, said: "Jim, you know, this is the last of May—it's just a spring shower; by ten o'clock tomorrow I'm sure we'll see some sunshine." Trout fishermen are ever optimistic, and such is the reputation of Deep Creek that we knew, regardless of rain, it would be unspoiled and no more than a little angry at most. It is appropriate here to mention Mark Cathey, who will be discussed in another chapter, for without him any story of Deep Creek would seem incomplete. I little thought that by the following afternoon we would see trout rising swiftly to Mark's dry fly.

I listened to the discomforting spatter of the rain draining from the eaves into a puddle below the window, wondering about the coming morning. "Jim," the Captain said, "I think Deep Creek is the grandest stream in the Smokies. In some ways it reminds me of those gin-clear English streams. Tomorrow we'll have another opportunity to watch Mark Cathey do his stuff. You know, the people around this part of the country just don't know how good the old man is." It was the same story I had heard many times—people just didn't know what a great angler Mark was. "Deep Creek's Mark's favorite stream, you know—he's lived most of his life on it and knows every pool and pocket from one end to the other." Elements permitting, on the morrow we were to enjoy one of the great sights of the Smokies: old Mark dancing his yellow-bodied gray hackle on that grand stream.

The sun was slipping through the drifting clouds the next morning when we parked in the grove next to the warden's house. He was to drive us two miles upstream to the "turn-around," and it was there that we met Mark Cathey and a mountaineer, who was standing by with two pack-mules. While our packs were being roped on the mules for the eight-mile trip upcreek, I walked over to the first ford to look at the water. It was as clear as though no rain had fallen, and what a stream it was,—coming down over the rocks, easing into a trouty-looking flat stretch before emptying into a deep pool, not less than a hundred feet in length.

Soon the mule pack took the lead up a sharp ridge to the right of the creek, and our four-man party followed afoot. By this ridge route we would come down to the creek trail a mile and a half upstream, thus avoiding the two lower fords, which were deeper and a little fast and angry that morning. On the crest of the ridge Mark Cathey stopped and, pointing between two trees, marked the spot where years ago, when he was a young man, his first wagonload of fingerling trout had overturned, taking the team, fish, and all down over the steep ridge into Deep Creek far below.

When our party arrived at the third ford, the two mules and their driver, who had momentarily dismounted, were waiting. We helped him raise the packs higher on the backs of the mules, and the first crossing began. The sure-footed animals well knew that the time had come to cross, but were in no hurry to plunge in. After a little encouragement by a few nudges in his flank the saddle-mule stepped cautiously into the shallow water. As the follow-up mule came up by his side, they both put their heads down as if to survey the slippery rocks of the deeper water ahead. While not refusing, they hesitated again, seeming to sense that the water was running fast and high. A little more nudging and they moved in with heads down; it was a slow, feeling start. But once they got the feel of the rocks under their steel-calked shoes it was something to watch, as they made their way side by side across this more than belly-deep ford. Reaching the other side, the fellow in the saddle called back, "This'n's the worst of the ten fords; it'll be easy going on up."

Continuing upstream that morning, we came to an interesting little tributary that slipped in quietly through the rhododendron and other bank growth, as if not wishing to be announced. Mark Cathey recounted his many trips up the small tributary for the rainbows and brookies it held, and how, there being no room for rod play, it was smart to "snake 'em out quick" if you wanted to put the fish in your basket.

Up above, Deep Creek began to take on a more peaceful aspect. With the sun streaming through the forest, the water looked friendly and inviting. Now, well on our way, we continued along the clearly marked streamside trail, leaving it only to cross the creek and pick it up again on the other side. Deep tracks in the occasional soft spots of black earth indicated that our mule pack was making satisfactory progress ahead. All along, beautiful pools and flat stretches were visible both ways from the fords. At each of them I paused in midstream, tempted by an occasional rise to assemble my rod, but our camping spot still lay well ahead and there was little time if we were to enjoy the better fishing higher upstream. Finally the tenth ford was crossed and we were on the last lap—a half mile more and we would be at camp.

It was midafternoon when we heard a mule snort. Looking ahead through an opening between the trail and a flat stretch of stream just above the Bryson Place, we saw our duffel neatly arranged on the ground. After a short rest and a very timely and potent refresher, we proceeded to put the camp in order. This was upper Deep Creek, in the very heart of the wilderness that is so typical of the Smoky country.

The ax is forbidden in the park, so we busied ourselves carrying in firewood from a stack provided under the direction of Uncle Sam's wardens a hundred yards from the camp. We younger men wanted Mark Cathey to rest and refused to let him help us, but someone said that we'd need trout for supper—and when we looked around, Mark was gone.

A bony black hound suddenly appeared from the forest, wagging a friendly tail. He soon began hungrily nosing our grocery sacks, whereupon all the provisions were swung high off the ground to the bough of a near-by red spruce. Well did the Captain remember how only the summer before, when he and Mark were camping at the same spot, a bear had carried away, and strewn up the mountainside, their stock of food and Mark's spare dry trousers, in which he had left a bag of salt.

Less than an hour had slipped by when we saw Mark coming through the bushes from the creek bank. His basket held a limit of trout. The Captain and Dr. Thomason, a fine angler, took one look at Mark's catch and were off upstream. I had missed what I most wanted to see: Mark Cathey in action. By all legal and moral laws he was finished for the day. Sitting there under the tarpaulin, Mark and

I came to a rather unusual agreement. I could probably take my limit before supper, just as I had intended to do. Why not, however, put into operation in this one instance a little underwritten law—which we both would forget when the day was spent? The ten rainbows in his basket could be *my* fish, as far as the world about us was concerned, and I could then have the privilege of watching him dance his fly to ten more fish. We agreed upon this happy arrangement, which, so far as the stream was concerned, would not vary the trout population.

I followed him out to the stream and for the next hour was merely an observer while old Mark, clearly showing his advanced age, treated me to an amazing performance with the dry fly. He reminded me somewhat of a boy playing with a toy while dancing his fly over the pockets among the rocks, in an unorthodox style peculiarly his own, giving the impression of an insect trying to rise from the surface of the water but never being quite able to do so. Performing as only the true artist can, in a stretch of water near camp that didn't look too attractive, he also proved that Deep Creek held its full share of trout.

The following morning two of us were to fish upstream, while the Captain and I planned to work the beautiful water between the fords below. This would be a good day, I believed, to try out a lure of my own making, one that I was sure would take trout. When I arrived at the eighth ford that morning, the water looked so intriguing that I decided to take to the stream there and fish down. The run of the water was particularly favorable to wading near the left bank, casting across to the right bank or to midstream as conditions indicated. With ideal water and weather conditions, I started with a rather large fly that the Captain had advised contained too much white for rainbow trout. I was not long in finding that he was right. While I seemed to be getting the maximum action out of the fly, still I didn't take fish. But, as is my way with lures, I was determined to stick with this fly that I had so carefully designed. As I fished down toward the next ford, I decided Deep Creek was living up to its reputation. Trout were in evidence at almost every spot where the fly was offered; never before or since have I brought so many trout to a fly without being able to hook a single fish. They would flash out, look it over, and return to their hiding-place. On several occasions when returning the fly to a trout that had come out swiftly (as if he meant business) on the initial cast, he would come again and look it over, but not so fast and with more caution each time.

Just below the seventh ford I was encouraged for a brief moment. My fly had seemed to settle right on the nose of a good trout. He struck, and for a second I thought I was fast to him, but in another second he was gone. I guessed that the fish got the fly into his mouth before he had time to look it over and without really intending to do so. By the time I had reached the sixth ford I was finished with that fly—it had been refused too often. But here was something for thought; it had one virtue: though utterly rejected, it really brought those Deep Creek trout out to have a look. My conclusion was that while the action was enticing enough, there was something wrong with the size and color.

On my way back to camp about midday, I came up with Captain, who had paused for a rest by the streamside trail. Throughout the morning he had taken trout consistently (releasing most of them) with two patterns of elongated woolly worm that he had used alternately. The two patterns that had proved most effective were tied on a No. 10 long-shanked hook, one of them with a salmon-colored body, the other with a body of light brown, both bodies tied with a soft fuzzy yarn, heavily shouldered with a trimming of light-brown hackle. While Captain was a confirmed dry-fly man, he occasionally fished wet, and for two seasons now he had proved these two combinations of the woolly worm to be consistent takers on Deep Creek.

We walked into camp and found our two companions already there; they had each netted some nice fish and were taking things easy for the remainder of the day. That night we enjoyed a grand meal of deliciously browned trout, turned only once in the pan of bacon fat by the skilled hand of Mark Cathey, and the other delicacies that make the fisher's camp meal complete. The forest warden, checking the stream on horseback, stopped by for a chat and, while eating a crisp browned trout and hot cornbread, gave us news of how the fishermen were doing up and down the creek. By this time the hound dog had made himself a member of the party and was displaying an uncanny accuracy at receiving table scraps. If he saw it coming—a fish head or a corn cake—it had no chance of touching the ground.

On the morning of the third day our party split up. Mark Cathey preferred the water near the camp. Captain Gatewood and Dr. Thomason went upstream and downstream respectively. I decided to take the trail up to the right prong of Deep Creek, a mile away, and begin there. This right fork comes down, crystal-clear, from the higher peaks of the Smokies, and here a woolly worm replaced the fly that I had fruitlessly toiled with the previous day. Right away two acceptable trout were taken from a broad flat stretch of water situated on the first bend of the prong. Wading on up, I came into a long, narrow pool, deep across from me, but shallowing off abruptly on my wading side. Among the many small trout I saw in this long pool, there were several good fish, but I failed to take one. I knew why. Overhanging growth on my side made it a difficult stretch for deceptive casting, and small fish darting along up-pool gave the danger signal to any good fish that might have been taken; thus, a care·· less approach had spoiled the pool. I planned another try at that pool later in the day.

Farther up, the stream narrows into closer confines, with numerous small pools, miniature falls, and abrupt turns and only an occasional eddy in the precipitous flow from the steeper region above. The trout ran smaller than in the lower waters but were more numerous—the way they raced each other for that woolly worm was quite interesting. But to put a ten- to twelve-inch fish in my creel it was necessary to approach carefully the dark spots of water that cut in under the bank, or a rock or a small eddy, where a better fish had more or less taken over. Toward midday two fishermen came along and passed me on their way farther up. I was still thinking of that long pool at the lower end of the prong, and it seemed a good time to retrace my steps. I needed two more trout to give me a limit. Not that a limit was important, but my showing had been negligible so far, and as we would break camp the following morning, I wanted to complete the day with something substantial. To take small fish near the minimum length would have been easy even for a novice, but I needed better than that.

A short while later I entered the stream just below the tail of the long pool, where it fanned out into the flat stretch. There I paused. There were miles of attractive water where good trout could be taken, but I wanted to feel the satisfaction—known only to fishermen —of conquering the long pool. I had seen what would happen by starting up the shallow side. Instead, I waded into the opposite side just below where the deeper water tailed off, careful not to disturb any small trout in the lower water. A cast up the left bank brought a strike from a barely legal-sized trout, which was returned. The second cast, a little higher, netted a beauty. The final trout of the day was taken when I crawled through the bushes about the center of the pool and from my knees executed a roll cast that placed the woolly worm seemingly right on top of a good fish. It was a fair example, I thought, of the various alternatives that may be employed on a difficult pool. Indeed, that morning on the right prong of Deep Creek was one not soon to be forgotten.

We spent the early part of the bright sunny morning of our last day on the stream getting the duffel packed for the return of the mules and their driver. The black hound, still hanging around, had been fed for the last time and seemed to sense that he must find new friends and a new campfire.

On this last day we planned to fish down between the fords—those broad stretches of the creek which were known to hold, not so many, but larger fish. The interesting part began when we first crossed the stream. Old Mark paused to dance his fly over a submerged log just above the ford. He tied into a good trout, but it tangled his leader about the log and was lost.

Going on down, our party broke up, preferring to fish the between-ford stretches singly. From ford to ford as we came in contact with each other, our baskets were gaining weight; rather from the size of the fish, however, than from their numbers. As I started to enter the creek a mile or more from the "turn-around" in the early afternoon, that black hound appeared in the trail behind me. He seemed to remember that I had not been unkind to him. As he gave me a good-by wag of his tail, the forlorn expression on his face indicated that he knew *this* crossing of the stream was final.

One by one, our party gathered at the "turn-around." It was near midafternoon. The warden was waiting with his truck. It had been a good day, a sunny May day in the Smokies, a day when the trout weren't too selective. Using different lures, we all had taken good trout, not a few up to sixteen inches.

Deep Creek is an almost ideal dry-fly stream, yet its trout are equally receptive to the usual variety of frauds, including the various wet-fly and spinner combinations. The food supply of both surface and stream-bed insects is ample. Rainbow trout inhabit both the lower and upper waters, but in the upper reaches the brookies are also in evidence here and there. Indian Creek, or one or two of the upper prongs, may be found closed for restocking, but during season there is always abundant water for all. In all the Smokies there are few finer streams.

CHAPTER III

Hazel Creek

With no stream in the Smokies am I more intimately acquainted than with Hazel Creek. This comes from some twenty years crowded with memories of golden days spent on this stream and its tributaries. Many unforgettable things come to mind; so many, in fact, that it is difficult to separate the grain from the chaff. But of all my fishing days none remain fresher than those on Hazel Creek. In outlining the quality and character of this fine rainbow-trout stream, renowned for almost thirty years, it seems proper to begin with a review of how it first caught the fancy of local anglers at a time when fishing clubs were something that Southerners just read about.

In the early twenties a group of western North Carolina sportsmen became possessors of a vast boundary on this creek. The property, which lies in the southwestern belt of the Smoky Range, became prominently known as the Hazel Creek Fishing Club. Those were the days of low-price acreage, and there were many streams to select from, offering fine possibilities; but after many days of stream and boundary investigation Hazel got the nod.

When first organized the club was exclusive, but with the passing years the stream was shared with local anglers. Realizing that their own fishing would make little dent in the more than thirty miles of water with its great numbers of trout, the owners were generous with those fellow anglers who plied the artificials. The creek became known as the finest stream in the Southeast. Today it is not questionable when old-timers relate how they creeled the limit from a single pool or from a certain section of the flat-water stretches without moving more than a step or two.

Of the many things that occur to me, few are more indelibly retained than my first and last trips, separated as they were by a span of more than twenty years. When I first saw this creek, I was little more than a youth, just beginning to take trout fishing seriously. On this first trip, with three others, I was the guest of my uncle Jim Stikeleather, one of the founders of the Hazel Creek Club. Late one Saturday afternoon we pulled up to the lower clubhouse, which had been prepared for this initial spring coming of trout fishers. That evening I was the last of our party to wade into the creek some seventy-five yards below the knoll on which the clubhouse was situated. As I entered, my uncle was leaving the stream. In little more than half an hour, he had taken all the trout he wanted. I fished in the identical smooth stretch of flat water he had retired from, a beautiful reach that glided along invitingly for perhaps a hundred feet. I remember well the two wet flies, a leader of inferior gut, and a line and rod of mediocre quality. What still lingers of this first experience is that in the little while before darkness ten rainbow trout were creeled from this same flat glide.

Of all my numerous trips, that first evening's fishing and my last, in August 1944, stand out most prominently. On this last visit to Hazel I was again the guest of my uncle. With us were two other anglers, one from New York City, the other from Florida. Again it was on a Saturday when we arrived at the clubhouse, its massive poplar log construction looking little different from the first time I had seen it. Conditions seemed very unfavorable. Coincident with our arrival about the worst trout weather one could imagine for the month of August was developing. It had rained as we came in—a cold rain—one of those preseason cold snaps which sometimes come early in the high mountains.

Soon we were all toasting by a roaring log fire in the living-room. With a chilly rain falling steadily, there seeemed little prospect of a profitable fishing afternoon. Realizing that it would perhaps be my last trip to the club property for some time—a year or two, maybe—I wanted to get all of the creek I could. Giving no notice of my intention, I got busy on the porch that separates the sleeping- from the lounging-quarters, selecting just the items of tackle suitable for such a day. Shortly, with a hooded rain jacket put to good use, I slipped down to the creek. Aside from the rain that slightly peppered its surface, the old glide looked about the same. Time had changed it little, and—characteristic of Hazel—there was no evidence of dingy water. With two woolly worms attached to the leader, one more than I would use under normal conditions, I started casting into the glide. Regardless of the continuous rain and unfavorable east wind, for some reason I felt that a trout or two could be taken. It was about the third cast, out into the middle of the glide where the water was deeper, that the first strike came. While I was playing this first strike, another trout fastened onto the dropper worm. I only realized that two were on when I saw them both come together near the surface of the water. They were both creeled without the use of a net. This start was a pleasant surprise.

For nearly an hour I stayed there on the glide; it wasn't necessary to go up or down stream. Without moving more than a few paces one way or the other I finished with ten trout, and six of those I kept came—as did the first two—by way of a double. Everything considered, it was far better than expected. Many times I have reminisced about the experience of those two far-separated days on the clubhouse glide. The take on those two occasions at the spot where I first waded into the creek was equal, but on that last rainy evening the trout came much larger.

It was a good example of how the fishing had held up over the long span of years. Throughout this whole period there has been little change in the creek's trout population. Regardless of the years when it was fished hard, there were no subsequent tough years, and this can be attributed to a splendid food supply and the many feeder streams available for fall spawning.

As dry-fly water, Hazel ranks at the very top. Few good dry-fly men have been defeated during late May or in June, July, and August. As on any stream, skill is a factor that counts when two or three dry-fly fishers are working equally good water. I'm reminded of a day, a typical dry-fly day, when a good friend of mine and another man from the North were fishing dry on the lower waters. There was a wide difference in the ability and experience of these two, the former possessing greater skill with the dry fly. The one well knew and enjoyed using the many refinements sometimes so essential on a gin-clear stream. The other loved to fish but took his fishing less seriously, resigned to the hit-or-miss philosophy. In the evening my friend wound up with a basket of beautiful trout selected from over a hundred rises. His companion came in with three uncomplimentary specimens that hardly qualified as "keepers." Looked at from another angle, the failure was due to a cheap mess of tackle difficult to manage, and to lack of knowing where to put the fly.

To this superlative dry-fly stream many personages have been attracted from various parts of the country, including some of America's best-known anglers. Ferris Greenslet comes to mind as one who has fished more trout waters than most in his day. On the lower waters of Hazel some years ago he had the gratifying experience of encountering a heavy hatch of Blasturus Cupidus at the very height of a thunderstorm, during which, in twenty minutes, he took eight fine-conditioned rainbows running from eleven to fourteen inches, all with one of Hewitt's Grey Bivisible No. 12's. This is just one of many experiences by which the creek became widely known, and why in books it has been mentioned so often as one of the great Southern streams.

Happenings on this stream of consuming interest to trout fishermen are too numerous to recount here, but there is one that still stands out with me—the rare and charming performance of three juvenile poachers. It happened while John Taintor Foote and his brother were guests of the club, although it wasn't disclosed until some time afterward. During their stay a huge trout was taken, but not by means of rod, reel, and line. On the second day of this particular trip two club members and the Foote party were fishing the main stream. This proved so fruitful that the smaller tributaries did not interest them. Nevertheless, one tributary—the little creek that flows through Bone Valley—was being fished. On the morning of this day one of the wardens was patrolling downstream. Coming to Bone Valley, he stopped. There were fresh footprints in the sand. They led upcreek. The evidence indicated that they were juvenile anglers—two or three of them, since the footprints were not uniform in size. Furthermore, he could see that they were barefooted. Since things like this were part of his job, he decided to go up and run them out. They were some youngsters from down at Proctor, he thought, and he knew Stikeleather wouldn't like that.

Some distance up the tributary he came to a bend in the stream. He stopped suddenly—he was looking at a strange performance he'd never seen before. Just ahead two small girls were lying on the edge of the creek with their heads and shoulders just out of the water and their arms locked together. He was not long in guessing the purpose of that maneuver, for they were lying right across the mouth of a small strip of backwater. It was one of those combinations of backwater pockets and eddy. In the pocket a boy was half wading and half crawling, lunging now and then in an effort to catch something—perhaps a bullfrog, the warden thought. Whatever he was after, it was evident the little girls were lying across the mouth of the pocket to prevent the prey from getting into the main stream.

Presently the boy was down on all fours feeling around the bottom. By that time the water was somewhat muddied. An instant later a huge trout was in the air. In an attempt to escape the pocket where he was cut off, the trout made a long leap in the direction of the stream. He almost landed in the arms of the little girls, and a second later the boy joined them, trying frantically to hold down the fish in water too shallow to swim in. In a flash they had him. After much commotion, in a few seconds the boy struggled to the bank, his arms locked around the fish in a death grip.

The warden waded across the stream for closer observation. Before him stood the boy holding a buckling rainbow trout that was all of four pounds.

For a moment the boy and the little girls were apprehensive, afraid the warden would take their precious fish. The girls looked about seven and nine years old, the boy eleven or twelve perhaps; they were brother and sisters. With assurance that no harm would come from the big uniformed warden, the boy explained just how it all came about. His story summed up like this:

He had been fishing upstream with worms while his sisters followed along. When he came to the bend, he saw something moving around in the pocket of water at the edge of the stream. Approaching closer, he saw it was a big fish. From there on, the boy had it all figured out. He eased across the stream quietly. When he reached the mouth of the pocket, he saw he could stretch his body lengthwise across it and cut the trout off. He did just that, but it was too big a job for his smaller sisters to catch the fish, though they tried desperately. Eager to succeed in this momentous undertaking, he placed his sisters across the point of egress and went after the trout himself. He had chased the fish about over the pocket for some time and once or twice had almost got him in his arms, but the fish was too slippery to hold. It was just after the warden came up that the fish was chased into a position where he could be finally captured.

Speaking to the boy, the warden said: "Son, you take that fish and get on down the creek. If you don't talk, that's one trout Jim Stikeleather will never know about."

There's still a little more about this stream that may well be included here. Little has been said about its several tributaries. In addition to Bone Valley, which comes in on the north side of Lower Hazel, there is Walker's Creek, which slips in on the same side four miles higher up—one of those picturesque streams enclosed by heavy vegetation, where one must shorten one's line if trout instead of twigs, limbs, and boughs are to be hooked. For the first mile rainbows are predominant, but from where a few hunky logs begin to block the smooth flow and make it difficult for them to get on up, the native brook trout take over. As little streams go, it is one of my favorites.

Farther up, Proctor Creek comes in from the northeast. From early to late season this has been one of the stream's most productive tributaries. Still farther up, the main stream separates into several lofty prongs where the fish hold their size and numbers remarkably well.

Of all the trout streams fished over a lifetime, this can be said of Hazel Creek: it has never defeated me completely. I have never started in any stream or tributary with less doubt of success.

When the season of 1944 ended, the owners of the Hazel Creek Club were reluctant to give up their stream, but they had no alternative. At the close of the season, title passed to the Great Smoky National Park, and along with other Smoky streams it is now open in season, but under park supervision.

CHAPTER IV

Other Smoky Streams

To evaluate a stream on the basis of popularity instead of its fish-carrying capacity, average size of fish, or any other one thing can only be confusing to the discriminating angler, who always has his own ideas about trout streams. Experience teaches that an individual trout stream may become popular either because it is easy to reach by auto or because it is easy to negotiate for much of its length; or it may be the beauty of its pools or their frequency; or because it gives many trout, though not large ones, to the basket. On the other hand, some fancy a stream that is remote for the very reason it is remote—'way back from any travelable road, and to be reached only the hard way. Such a stream is often relied on for better trout. The angler who tramps his way up and in to such water does so because, to him, one or two fifteen- to sixteen-inchers—and maybe, yes, maybe, a duplicate of that twenty-two-incher he netted last season—will give more satisfaction than a basket of eight- to twelve-inchers. Anyway, on the Tennessee side there are various streams of distinction of this kind.

Little River, easily reached by motor, as well as being the largest is perhaps the most popular, generally, of all trout streams that drain on the Tennessee side. In addition to its excellent tributary prongs, which offer good rainbow and brook fishing, the main stream offers fair rainbow fishing for its entire length. However, the natives on that side favor the water above the Limestone Sinks, and there is a lot of water above the sinks, which the angler will not be long learning about if he chooses to cast to the pools and glides of this fine stream.

In this same class are the middle and west prongs of Little Pigeon River. Like Little River, they are two favorites of the native fisherman, and many non-native anglers have found these streams so much to their liking that, season after season, they have paid them return visits. The lower stretches of the two prongs afford excellent rainbow water, and splendid brook-trout fishing is offered in the head waters of these prongs.

About twenty years ago I first learned about Abrams Creek, another stream that is splendid trout water, which drains down the western side of the Smokies. Abrams is fished less than most other Smoky streams, as it is not so well known, but those who do know its quality as trout water regard it highly. This creek came to my attention in the mid-twenties when four camping fishermen came out from Abrams with a catch of rainbow that averaged more than a pound per fish. Twenty years is a long time with any trout stream; changes for better or worse can easily take place, but since the twenties on through to the present time the rainbow of this creek, according to those who fish it most and know it best, come larger than from any other stream on the Tennessee side of the Smokies. Not that big trout don't come from other streams; they do, particularly from the prongs of Little River and Little Pigeon River; but Abrams in proportion to the amount of fishing there gives a greater number of trout running from fourteen to twenty inches than any other individual stream.

This creek is known as the camper's stream. It is situated on the west end of the Smokies, where the good roads give way some distance from the stream to a rougher traillike country, too rough and far away to suit the convenience of the easygoing fisherman, but most inviting to the camper, who likes to put up for a few nights by the streamside, usually in the vicinity of Abrams Falls. To the credit of some anglers going to this trout water, they voluntarily put a limit of twelve inches on their fish, which is indicative of how the trout grow there. In addition to rainbow, the higher prongs present some of the best brook-trout water in the Smokies. It is the old story again: fine trout water that is taxing on the physical reserve, but that, once reached, has its rewards. For camping fishermen who like such conditions no stream in the Smokies is more promising. From this corner, it is highly recommended during late May on through August as the camping fisherman's dream.

The trout streams so far individually treated are generally considered the best in the Smokies. They are given preference here because they are most inviting, especially to anglers unfamiliar with park streams as a whole or with other streams that offer occasional good fishing, but only at some particular season. Within the park boundaries, on both the North Carolina and the Tennessee side, other streams offer good fishing also; for example, Big Creek, flowing down from the northeastern tip of the park. This is a high-up stream where a 16 or 18 dry fly is often the only answer in late June, July, and August. In the warmer season you will see many trout in its crystal waters, but find it difficult to take even one good fish unless you have just the right fraud and know how to present it.

As a good example of what this stream is often like, I am reminded of three anglers I sent there not so long ago. After camping on the creek overnight, two of the anglers fished it hard the following day, using every trick of trout fishing known to them, but without result. Many trout could be seen, but because of the extreme clarity of the water it was almost impossible for these two to make a cast and remain undiscovered. The third angler, an excellent dry-fly man, did business with the trout by resorting to an extra-fine leader and a size-18 dry fly. (Many times I've heard the same story, where small flies were the only answer.) Big Creek is water that some pass up on account of its reputation of being difficult, yet others fancy it for that very reason.

Oconalufty River is another delightful stream where trout fishing is good through much of the season. From the park boundary up several miles it is rainbow water, but the upper reaches contain both rainbow and speckled, thus giving a variety to the angler who likes the uncertainty of what may take. Oconalufty has several prominent tributaries that, as a rule, can be depended upon. They are Raven's Fork and its smaller tributaries, Stilwell Creek and Straight Fork, and Bradley Fork, a sizable tributary of the main river. In the tributary prongs, especially high up, both rainbow and brook trout are found. Since the Oconalufty is easily accessible by auto and is fished hard during the early season, mid- and late-season fishing is often less fruitful. The best fishing I've experienced on this stream, however, was in the lower water—a three-mile stretch above the boundary—near the end of August, at a time when most anglers were working the waters farther up. As suggested, good fishing may be spotty after the first few weeks of the season, but it's a long stream with many miles of probable water to choose from.

Another rainbow and brookie stream is Forney Creek, with the brookie overlapping with the rainbow in the higher waters, as is characteristic of most park streams. My last day on this creek is well remembered. A nice basket of trout came from the lower two miles, just above where the creek then emptied into the Little Tennessee River—and at a time when the forest was being cleared from Lower Forney to make it ready for the impounding of Fontana Lake. Forney is a rather fast stream all the way down, and yet it contains many pools. It is good dry-fly water from late May through the remainder of the season. Since the creation of Fontana it is predicted that Lower Forney will offer better fishing and larger trout.

Eagle Creek and Twenty-Mile Creek—the former flowing into Fontana near the dam, the latter into Lake Cheoah a short way below—are two others that belong in the category of average trout streams. There is an old story dealing with Eagle Creek about which I have never been able to learn the true facts. In the upper waters fishing has never been very good—at least not in my day. In fact, there is one stretch of the upper water that seems to be almost entirely devoid of trout. That reminds me of one of the Smoky Mountains, Old Baldy, which has long been a mystery, for on it, above a certain elevation, it has definitely been established a tree will not grow. Anglers have told me about examining this stretch of water most carefully without being able to see so much as a single fish. One aging fisherman who has fished the park streams for almost forty years, back at a time when Eagle Creek could be reached only by foot, became curious enough about this strange strip of water to investigate it some years ago. He tells me—and this concurs with assertions of others—that in this particular upper stretch there is a mineral element that creates a toxic condition detrimental to trout. Such a condition might more easily be accounted for well below its source, but whatever the facts, lower Eagle is full of fish life. There, and also in lower Twenty-Mile Creek, many fine rainbow have come to net and still do.

Farther around on the western tip of the range, beyond the Appalachian Trail, which divides the Smoky boundary between the two states, there are several worthy streams other than those discussed in this chapter. Panther Creek and a tributary, Parsons Branch, are two that deserve mention. From a short distance above where it empties into the Little Tennessee River, six miles up, Panther Creek

Young Carl Grueninger Jr. with his first rainbow trout, caught in the Oconaluftee River, one of the streams Gasque covers, in 1939 or 1940, a few years after the creation of the national park and a few years before the publication of Gasque's book. The adult is a park ranger. The photo was taken by Grueninger's uncle, I. K. Stearns. (Image courtesy of Jim Casada)

R. Q. Woody Sr. of Bryson City stands on a bridge over Noland Creek, one of the streams Gasque covers, with a limit of trout he caught there on May 10, 1941. The English setter in the photo, Joe Ghost, belonged to the photographer, I. K. Stearns. Stearns was the literary executor of Horace Kephart. (Image courtesy of Jim Casada)

is good trout water. The lower half is rainbow water, but the rainbow overlap with brook trout in the upper half of the stream. Upper Panther Creek is hard going, but the trout are up there. Parsons Branch is short, but from Calderwood Lake, into which it empties, three miles up, it is a splendid brookie stream. It is rugged, but for the hardy angler the climb isn't too rough.

Aside from the streams discussed on both sides of the park, there are still other small streams and tributaries on which fair trout fishing is occasionally available, depending on stocking and other factors, and these will come in for an angler's attention if he spends much time in the Smokies.

ᴄ§ CHAPTER V §ᴇ

Little Streams

Where is the fisherman who does not have his favorite "little" stream —one typical, perhaps, of dozens in the neighborhood, but to him distinctively individual? A stream of unimportant manners, perhaps, yet holding memories that will remain always. That it has held, in its day, fair-sized trout may be no secret, but, what with the physical handicaps of maneuver and casting and the certainty of larger fish in the big water, such brooks are far too often disregarded by the average angler.

Some years back, a farmer I knew suggested that on my next trip out Smoky way I bring along a trout rod—he wanted me to fish a certain little stream that had some trout in it, a stream he claimed had not been fished for several years. At the time I was not impressed, but on my next trip I decided to accept his invitation, although with a skeptical mind.

The following Saturday I drove back to his farm. He was ready to go with me. Arrived at the stream, too small to have a name, he chose to sit in the car where highway and stream intersected, while I went up and fished.

"Well, that's the branch I was telling you about," he said; "go to it."

At once I was filled with misgiving. There was a culvert crossing under the road, but I could not see much stream. Walking over to the culvert, I did hear a trickle of water down under a mass of briers and other ditch-bank growth, but the first impression registered double minus.

"You've got to go on up—it gets bigger and widens out a piece up," he said.

It was evident that he sensed my disapproval at the ditchy-looking branch that seemed just about right for shiners. "It might widen out, but how can it increase in size as I go up?" I asked myself.

But to show some appreciation of his good intentions, I decided to go up anyway and kill some time, just to give it a try. I started up his so-called trout stream, breaking my way through bush and brush for two hundred yards to a point where things opened up just slightly.

Coming to a turn in the stream, I observed that it did carry more water than I first thought, but I was still apprehensive. Working up to a sharp bend, I stopped to observe a miniature pool that widened to perhaps four feet and was about six feet in length, just below a spot where the water turned *in under* the bank. There I decided to put a fly on and let the current carry it down—there was no other way to fish it. With three feet of leader and about four of line extending from the fly tip, I dropped in the fly. It had just passed the lip of the pool when a sharp tug registered up the rod. A fast retrieve brought an eight-inch rainbow—an agreeable surprise. I was inclined to think the fish just a lost little rainbow that had got in to the branch in some mysterious way. But at least it would evidence the fact I had fished.

After much straddling of bush and boughs—partly on all fours—in addition to retrieving my hat several times—I arrived at a fair opening in the stream. On above I could see several little pools and pockets. Here the stream broadened out considerably and was larger than I could have imagined, since the narrow swift water below was most deceiving with respect to the upper waters. Fishing several pockets and small pools, I was agreeably surprised to find trout taking at almost every spot where the fly was presented. Their size was anywhere from five to nine inches. That stretch gave me two legals, but I was having extreme difficulty in getting my hands on the fish. Once hooked, there was no room or place for the play; it was flip them to the bank, when, where, and if that could be done. Otherwise, unless well hooked, a few darts this way or that and the trout was free again.

After breaking through the brush for a short distance, I came to a stretch of water that offered definite possibilities ahead. The pools were growing in size as their numbers increased, but the question was how a fair take of rainbows could be brought to basket on that heavily overhung brook. Not that a full bag was all-important, but when one deserts the big water for that sort of rough going on a tiny tributary, one feels more deserving of some weight in the basket—at least I did. It was not a question of hooking the fish; the brooklet was delivering beautifully to the fly, but my eight-and-a-half-foot rod was much too long. It was impossible to keep a tight line, and the question becoming more manifest all along was how to complete the capture after setting the hook.

At the first pool I decided upon a tactic that served reasonably well. Thereafter I would take my time and write an individual ticket for each spot of water where the fly was to be presented. If there was a possible place to slide the fish out quickly or a spot of bank where capture might be accomplished, I'd start the rod tip in that direction the instant following the strike. Working slowly and carefully in this manner, I began to accumulate trout in the creel. They were hooked in nearly every likely spot, many of them too small, yet I got two more nice ones from eight to ten inches, and all exceptionally well conditioned.

Shortly I came to a series of stair-step falls. Looking up these falls, which fell perhaps seventy feet in a distance of something like a hundred, I wondered if a trout could be taken up there where the water on its way down poured from rock to ledge and so on. The broken formation of the solid rock offered good footing, and the possibilities beckoned me on. The pool at the bottom of the falls gave me a fat fish. Climbing on up, the next pool held a good one, but he was on only a second or two, then off to hide under his rock. A surprising volume of water pooled up at the bottom of each fall.

Farther up I came to a strip of inkish water about two feet wide, shaped as it was by two cratering rocks situated crosswise of the broken stream for a length of perhaps twelve feet. The water emptied, funnel-like, to the extreme right from the supporting rocks. A small pool just above poured its crystal waters down into this narrow strip. A rainbow flashed in the pool above, but I was possessed with a desire to toss my fly across to the end of the dark water and retrieve back to my side. For concealment's sake, I was on my knees before and when the fly was presented. The fly had scarcely touched the water when there was a sharp tug; the rod tip went down and toward the far side. I wanted *that* trout—this time there was real weight on the other end. Like a flash the fish was back and forth across the narrow strip of water several times. On the fifth or sixth run in my direction I helped him along, swiftly skidding him out of the water onto the steep sloping bank. There he was, motionless, the fly out of his mouth. A flop or two would put him safely back into the water. Instantly I dropped the rod and was upon him, my body and arms between him and the stream. For so little a stream, he was indeed a prize. I was thrilled at taking that rainbow as I would be by a twenty-incher from a larger stream. He had a beautiful deep color, was fat, and measured thirteen inches. From there on up

I began releasing legal trout, holding back for one just a little larger since I was nearing my limit.

Above the falls the stream opened up beautifully and was less difficult to follow. Up there the flow of water seemed slower; I was surprised at the volume stored in the pools. It was beginning to look like one of the secret little streams that are sometimes whispered about. Several times I actually found room to cast instead of tossing the fly, but still it was necessary to plan in advance just how each fish should be maneuvered if he was to go into the creel. Working the better water to good advantage till I again came to a rough overgrown territory, I needed only one more trout for my basket. Crossing a log, I was down low, working my way under the low-hanging bank growth to the next opening. My rod tip was pointed upstream, with about two feet of leader trailing from it. Unknown to me, the fly had carelessly dropped into a dark little pool and the rod tip suddenly tugged, then jerked. Right there the last trout was hooked so fast I simply laid the rod to one side and crawled up to the flopping fish. This brought an end to the afternoon—one of rugged going, but nevertheless highly interesting.

This was not the end, however, for me on that stream. Confident that I could do a better job after my first experience, I was back again the following week-end. Again some forty trout of various sizes took my fly, making it an easy matter to select a nice bag of fat fish.

For two summers I fished this water, which looked no more than a weedy branch where it crossed under the highway. On each occasion the take was commensurate with the effort.

This streamlet is a fair sample of many of its kind in this mountain region. It is typical of those that are passed up either as too difficult to fish or as more or less worthless. While this is a rainbow stream, it can be truly said that some of the grandest little brook-trout streams in Eastern America slip along modestly through the higher Appalachians.

Experience with such water has convinced me that trout in small streams take better and more consistently than in the larger waters, and often their size compares favorably with that of those from the larger streams. I merely emphasize the value of lesser waters and what they will give to the basket when worked diligently. They may serve better than expected on those occasions when the larger streams are running full, or when, in July and August, they get tough.

In small streams there is one thing definitely in the angler's favor, and in this they are all alike. In such water it is a simple matter to determine just where the fish are; each little pool, pocket, eddy, or run will hold its individual trout, sometimes two or even three. There is less error in small-stream tactics when they are applied skillfully. And something else: to get the best from them, one doesn't have to assemble one's gear before dawn; almost any time of day may be equally profitable.

Often one hears that a spinner or spinner fly is not practical for tiny streams. That may possibly be so, but here are the facts as I have found them. I know nothing more killing than a *small* spinner, Colorado or Idaho shape, when attached to a small fly or woolly bug. I will not go into this at length except to say that when the small spinner is tossed in and brought across tiny pools and pockets, the trout certainly do dart out and take for me. Many times in spots of water not larger than the family bathtub I have tossed a spinner fly on the sand to one side or the other, and as it was drawn through the water have had a trout take it before it had traveled a foot. The wet fly is, of course, similarly effective, as it is a natural for that kind of fishing. As for the dry fly, I hardly know what to say. The neophyte would be lost on the miniature stream with a floater. However, many trout can be snatched out by just dabbing or skittering a dry-fly across the likely spots. Sometimes they will take the instant it touches the water; but wet flies usually serve more satisfactorily. Another thing about the trout of little streams: they seem more avid than those of larger waters. Frequently the same fish (sometimes after he has seen you) will take and take again and most willingly until he is hooked, provided he is not unduly frightened.

Among the many such streams I think of one in particular: Little Walker's Creek in the Great Smokies, a tributary of Hazel Creek that, high up, one can step across in places. I remember many things about that stream, including the rainbow and brookies it has given me, and a tobacco pouch that was once carried down a fast ripple.

In the Smokies are many little streams where the timber is virgin, where the water is as fresh and limpid as it was a hundred years ago. There is that something about them which will always recall pleasant memories. With their soft curling currents, darkish bank cavities, and continuous chain of pools and pockets, they offer, in miniature, untold delightful surprises. In July or August one is glad to absorb some of their cool freshness and also the sunshine streaming through the high forest, and not worry about one's income tax or the grocer's bill. Yes, little streams do have their charms.

CHAPTER VI

Mark Cathey

By special design I give this final chapter on trout fishing in the Smokies to Mark Cathey. Not to do so would be a significant omission. It may be said without fear of contradiction that from the nineties to the early forties Mark Cathey was the greatest dry-fly fisherman of the Smoky region.

A lifelong resident of the Deep Creek section near the town of Bryson City, he had the face of the mountaineer. Practically all of his adult years were devoted to fishing and hunting in his native mountains, so his life was vitally tied in with the Great Smokies. His reputation as a dry-fly artist must ever remain at the very top with living anglers native to his countryside. Every region has its champion fisherman, but Mark must be classed as a champion of champions. His name was widely known; anglers from many states came to fish with him and to see him fish in his unique one-man style. Hundreds of the faithful agree that during his lifetime no other angler in North Carolina or Tennessee could approach him in limit catches day after day throughout the years, or in the brief time normally taken to displace air in his basket. This is not to say that he was one to boast of his limit catches; he was never a man for that. A limit, to him, was more a matter of habit or a place to stop than something to preserve a reputation or something to attain. There are so many tales of this unusual character and his highly unorthodox but effective manner of employing the dry fly that not a few of the younger generation of anglers are attempting to master his style. This, and that he had no peer in his special field, and that for more than fifty years he was so closely associated with the wild life of the Smokies, are why it is a delight and an inspiration to write about him.

Many were the occasions on which he admirably sustained his remarkable reputation, and the best way to reveal how he came by it is to go back many years and show him in action. This was at a time when Mark Cathey was in the prime of life. Though quite unaware of any audience, he was putting on a spectacular performance before a Tennesseean who had recently taken over a cabin in an isolated locality on the south side of the Smokies, and this cabin fronted on a small trout stream.

One evening the Tennesseean, looking downstream, saw a man snake a good trout from one of his small pools. A minute later another was taken from the same pool, and then a third was hooked and netted from the same spot. The Tennesseean was not long in realizing his stream was being "cleaned." The stranger was getting three for every one the Tennesseean had been able to take.

For the moment the fellow's art with a fly took precedence over the stream's heavy loss, and he held his peace, content to watch the peculiar method of dry-fly maneuvering bring one trout after another out from hiding. The stranger fished on up and soon neared the point where the owner was standing. Never had he seen a stream so completely stripped in such an unorthodox fashion. All his good trout were being hooked not over twenty feet from the stranger as he jigged and danced his dry fly on the surface all about him without any apparent effort to retrieve. He retrieved only when a fish was on, but that was frequent. It was a distinct departure from the conventional method of making the cast and allowing the fly to float down the current—an individual method that the owner had never seen before, though he was quite an angler himself.

He was gazing at a genius taking trout with a style scarcely credible, a style in which trout presumably just couldn't be taken. He saw him bring out one wary trout three times without the trout taking, but he continued dancing that fly over the same fish until the sale was made. The stranger fished on up, pulling fish out of every pocket holding one, making the fly do a beautiful dance back and forth over the fish, sometimes right at his feet, but never more than twenty feet in front or to the side, until the fish could resist the skippety-hop no longer. He and his rod were like one smooth-working machine, with the greater life coming from the bobbing fly instead of the machine that gave it life. From man to fly the three actions visible were a trembling hand, a shaking line, a dancing fly. The sportsman didn't know it, but he was seeing the master at his best. He was looking at the one and only Mark Cathey, originator of his own style—the dance of the dry fly.

The Tennesseean then stepped into the open. In his usual pleasant manner, Mark passed the time of day. He had seen no signs up, so he thought it all right to fish on through the newly acquired place.

"This is my water," the owner said, "and my trout, but go ahead and fish. You've got something worth watching—worth more than the trout, just to see you do it. This stream will be raped when you go out; you're really stripping it; but for that sort of fishing you can have them and welcome."

I pass on to another instance of his skill. On a June morning not many years ago Mark was on Forney Creek—on it just long enough to "net" a limit of rainbow trout. (He never used a landing net.) Arrived at the stream, he crossed Uncle Sam's boundary line and walked up to the bridge a hundred yards beyond. There at the end of the bridge he sat down for a short rest before beginning activities. The minutes passed and presently he heard shoe leather making contact with the gravel road upstream. Looking upstream, he saw a fellow angler coming round the bend.

He came on to the bridge where Mark was sitting, and soon the two were in conversation. He showed Mark his two trout, a skimpish eight inches, and began lamenting his poor luck. Mark looked at the two fish, then at the fellow, but didn't say much. Continuing the conversation, this man suggested that it was a poor day; the fish weren't taking. He'd fished hard since daylight and he had only two small fish for his hours of hard labor. The pay-off just wasn't worth the effort, he complained, looking Mark over with disdain as the aged angler sat there unassumingly in his rough but clean clothing. The conversation became more familiar and the stranger asked Mark: "How many you got?"

"My basket is empty," Mark replied.

"I'm not surprised," the man said. "Don't think you'll do much today."

"But I ain't fished yet," Mark said in his quiet way, and with that he pulled out his watch. It was then ten thirty. "By noon I'll have my leemit and be headed for Bryson."

To such a remark coming from a man who didn't look wise in the ways of angling, the stranger didn't have much to say, but thought he'd hang around a bit and see what the old man had on his mind.

Mark had no fears. The day before he had fished the same water, taking his "leemit" in an hour. From the bridge he had looked the stream over. While the man was advising and predicting, Mark had noticed an occasional rise here and there. Conditions were favorable; Mark had never felt more certain of doing just what he said he'd do. He never cared for an audience when fishing, but during his life hundreds had followed him on the stream. If this fellow wanted to watch, it was all right with him.

The man continued to express doubts that Mark could raise any fish as Mark began to rig up his rod. After it was jointed up, he took hold of the line and leader and began pulling them through the guides. While he was fingering his leader, the stranger inquired what kind of fly he intended to use.

"Just a plain dry fly; gray hackle with yellow body, I guess," was Mark's reply.

"Wait a minute; you'll never take trout on a leader that big," the stranger said. "It's big enough for bass. Haven't you got something smaller? I've got one in my box here that's much better. You'd beter put it on."

"Nope, I'll make out with this one all right," Mark replied.

Well enough did Mark know that his leader was larger than that ordinarily used. He well knew that the conventional dry fly demanded a very fine leader, but he was not doing that sort of dry-fly fishing. When Mark was ready to tie on a fly, he took from his pocket a small tin box holding half a dozen flies, 10's and 12's, brown hackles and gray hackles.

"Those won't do a' tall," the fellow said. "I tried those patterns this morning and they wouldn't raise a fish." And with that he pulled out a leather book containing dozens of frauds of every color in the rainbow. He began suggesting what and what not to use, advising this and that about color and the theory of simulating the insects on the stream.

Mark didn't care for all this talk—too much was enough. "Look here," he said, "how many fish you got in your basket? Two, that's how many. If you city fellows didn't fool with so much humbug, maybe you'd catch more fish. You've done the talking, now let me show you something. You got an hour to spare?"

"I guess so."

"All right, show the sorriest fly in your lot—one you think ain't no good."

With that the man picked out a .fly that he claimed had never raised a fish. "Don't know what you want with it," he said. "It's not worth a damn. But now here's a good one," and he picked up the one he had taken the two fish on. "Want to try it?"

"Nope, I'll take this one here that you say is no good. I don't usually argue with you dressed-up fishermen who carry around two or three hundred flies to look at, 'cause you don't pay no attention nohow; but today I'm feeling good and I'll just show you how much humbug there is to carrying round a lot of stuff you don't know how to use. My flies are better, but I'll just take this one and show you it'll catch trout, too."

Mark had looked the fly over; it was about a No. 12 of an off color he didn't like, but he knew it would take fish when it started dancing. He tied it on and headed for the stream, the other man following at his heels. At the bend of the creek just above the bridge, Mark stepped into the water and waded out until it reached his knees. The stranger had no conception of coming events; nor did Mark have an idea how easy a task he was to have. The day was fine, with conditions well-nigh ideal, and Mark was going to take time out to prove a few things to one who had frowned on his coarse leader and favorite gray hackle and who knew so much about trout fishing, yet couldn't produce himself. He was going to show that a plain countryman in blue overalls was capable of performing in convincing style where putting trout in the basket was a consideration. As he had often mused, those superfine woven theories were just humbug; at no time did he want more than three or four patterns of a fly, and size 10 or 12 was all for size so far as he was concerned.

Standing there in the water, Mark looked upstream toward a rock that broke water about midstream. The pocket below it would hold a trout—of that he felt sure. He possessed implicit confidence the moment he stepped into water—and rightly, too. He held out his rod and tossed the fly to the pocket. The instant it touched, he had it turning from one side to the other, dancing across the pocket like a struggling fly trying to rise from the surface. Now and then it would rise an inch or two above the surface, only to fall back with more skitter and dance. The fly gave a perfect impression of an insect trying desperately to take off, but never being able, seemingly, to do so.

Mark had danced the fly but a few seconds when a rainbow could stand it no longer and shot like an arrow from under the rock. After the fish had been played and taken, Mark looked back and said: "This colored-up fly ain't so bad, fellow."

Shortly he brought out another from the same rock and added it to the basket. When he could raise no more there, he waded on upstream a short distance to the tail of a pool and looked it over *very* carefully. There, from one position, he danced his fly until three more trout were placed in the basket. The other was watching with amazement, but did not venture further in an advisory capacity. At the head of the pool Mark took another; then he motioned to the fellow—who by this time had passed from instructor to student—to follow on. As he waded on upcreek the same performances were repeated, and in something like forty minutes his basket contained the limit of trout.

Mark untied the fly and handed it back to the other angler, saying: "Here, my friend, take it; it's all right, but not as good as

[47]

my gray hackles. Now remember, it ain't those fine leaders and two hundred flies colored like a store window, but the man behind the rod—that's what counts."

We come now to a June day in 1942, when he was leisurely fishing the lower waters of Deep Creek. About midday a strange angler came along, looked Mark over, and passed the time of day before continuing on upstream. That man was Captain R. D. Gatewood, a dry-fly angler of long experience who has been mentioned before. At this first meeting the Captain was little impressed with this aged man's unconventional method of dry-fly maneuver, but he watched him a couple of minutes before passing on. He didn't know it, but at that very moment Mark Cathey's basket had more weight in it than any basket on the creek. The Captain finished out the day with a total of four rainbow. He had fished with all he had, but it was a tough day for everyone on the creek, one man excepted.

Later in the afternoon the Captain arrived back at the place where the warden was taking the day's creel census; several had come in and others were following as the fishing day was drawing to an end. It was the same story with all—one of those tough days. The baskets held anywhere from one to three trout. Some of them had nothing. One or two had four, including Captain Gatewood's.

Watching the almost empty baskets as they were checked in, the Captain picked up a conversation going on between two natives. One was betting the other a dollar that old man Mark would come in with a limit catch. "I've never seen him fail," one said. "I'll put my money on him."

Then the warden spoke up. "I'll take another dollar on Mark if anyone wants it."

For a moment the Captain was inclined to offer a five-spot against this man Cathey. When he had fished a stream all day

Mark Cathey, near Deep Creek, 1944. (Courtesy of Jan Davidson)

The grave of Mark Cathey in the Bryson City Cemetery, which is located on a hill immediately southwest of the little mountain town. Cathey's gravesite lies just a few yards away from the boulder marking the final resting place of Horace Kephart, author of Our Southern Highlanders. (Image courtesy of Jim Casada)

long—offering everything he had with all the art and cunning acquired from fishing the world over—and when he had just four trout as a result, no man, he believed, could dry-fly a limit from Deep Creek on that particular day.

At that minute the old man came in sight up the trail. "We'll soon see," the warden said.

When Mark walked up, the fellow who had his dollar on him called out: "Got your limit, Mark?"

Mark looked at the man and answered: "Yes, I got my leemit, boys. How'd you fellows do?"

The Captain had a shock; he was looking at the old gentleman he had passed in the morning—and at a basketful of beautiful rainbow as fat and sleek as one could desire. "What did you take them with?" the Captain inquired.

"Dry fly," Mark said. "Want to see it?" Mark showed him his fly and equipment. He possessed a splendid rod, and his fly was all right—as usual, a gray hackle with yellow body. But the line was of poor quality and the leader three times as large as the Captain would use.

Well, that was something, he thought. We live and learn. He was glad he had kept his five dollars in his pocket. Mark explained that he had taken at least forty trout, but had carefully released the smaller ones, and those in his basket certainly evidenced the truth of his statement.

After he had checked his fish and gone on down the trail, Captain Gatewood questioned the warden further about the old man.

"Mark is the best in these parts," the warden told him. "It's hard to explain how he does it, but he gets 'em. I've never known him to come in without a limit when the weather was fit for fishing. That's a broad statement, but if you'll check on him you'll find it true."

So much for that, the Captain thought. But then he had a strong desire to see this man in action.

At five o'clock the following morning Captain hopped out of bed and turned on the light. He was going to find that fellow Cathey and see him fish. He knew he would never be satisfied till he did. His mind was made up—he would go over to Bryson City and locate that extraordinary fisherman.

Two hours later the figure of a man strolled past the window where he was having breakfast in a café. It was Mark Cathey, and the Captain flagged him. Mark seemed pleased that a strange angler wanted to see him fish. "Yes, I'll go fishing with you," he said. "You finish your breakfast. I'll get my rod and meet you in front of the Courthouse in thirty minutes."

An hour later they were standing on the bank of Deep Creek, the Captain in the capacity of a spectator only. Mark assembled his rod and waded out to a protruding rock near the tail of a pool. He took solid footing on it and looked things over. He tossed his fly some fifteen feet over by a rock in the lower end of the slow water and had it dancing the instant it touched the surface. In less than five seconds a trout was striking at it. One, two, and three times the trout tried to catch it. It seemed that Mark was purposely making the trout miss, thus demonstrating to his spectator that he could hold his fish to the spot by his unique tactic of dancing the fly in a figure eight on the surface. Presently he withdrew the fly, and the trout went back to cover. In a moment he brought the fish back out by doing the same thing again. This time he hooked and took the fish.

In all his fishing on both sides of the Atlantic, never had the Captain seen anything like that. Mark took three trout before moving from that pool, all in precisely the same manner. They moved on upstream. This time Mark selected a cluster of potato-like rocks situated in faster water averaging two to three feet deep. There he added three more fish to those in the basket, taking them all by just dancing the fly ten to fifteen feet in a circle from where he stood. He made the fly wobble and dance on the surface by an almost invisible wrist movement that kept the rod tip trembling and shaking constantly.

If only Edward R. Hewitt and George LaBranche could have been there, the Captain was thinking. These two great anglers of the North had many years before discovered that trout could be excited into a striking fervor if one possessed the ability to dance the fly artfully over the fish. It is so difficult, however, that few ever pursue this unconventional method to its perfection, but Mark was a past master of the art and had reached the pinnacle among a sparse handful of Americans known to use somewhat similar technique.

The two men moved on upstream. Again the old fisherman selected the tail of a smooth pool. He knew the trout of that stream and just where they would be lying, off feed or on. In a matter of minutes the Captain was treated to an amazing performance. Mark brought three or four trout from their hiding-places to his dancing hackle almost simultaneously. There was no question of the fish's seeing the angler. He was in plain view. But he had them so excited they were darting and rushing all over the place trying to catch a dancing bug that the old master wouldn't let them have until he was ready.

Turning to Captain Gatewood, he said: "See, they ain't afraid, Captin, when I get 'em excited. They just don't have time to notice *me*. See that good one going back under the rock over there? Now watch; I'll bring him out again, and this time I'll let him have it."

And so he did. Right there in that pool Mark finished out his limit. With his unique method he had put them to striking in a sort of frenzy, and one by one he dropped them in the basket.

There is one final story, and not to include it here would be to omit one of the most dramatic days of Mark's life. The events attending and climaxing his notable last performance will live long in the memories of those who saw it. The last week of August 1944 Jim Stikeleather had invited Captain Gatewood and me as his guests for this final trip of the season to Hazel Creek. I shall always regret that in this instance I let business take precedence over fishing.

About noon the next day the two men arrived in Bryson City. Turning right at the Courthouse, they headed down Main Street, whence they would turn to the Hazel Creek road. A moment later they spied Mark Cathey standing near the railway station. Old Mark was a happy man to see the Captain again. He remembered their days together and perhaps the felt waders, Hardy's English leaders, and others things the Captain had sent him. "Well, gentlemen, I'm glad to see you," he said: "I was just standing here wondering if I'd fish again this year. Season's over in a few days, you know. Where you going, Captain?"

After a few exchanges Mark accepted their invitation to go along to Hazel Creek, and in a matter of minutes the three men were off down the Little Tennessee River.

The following morning the Captain and Stikeleather held a conference. The Captain had a premonition that old Mark's fishing days were drawing to an end. Mark's physician had warned him that his heart was bad and that he should not take strenuous exercise. But he loved his fishing too much to give it up and paid little attention to any doctor. For several years now he had been taking his walking-stick into the stream while he fished, bracing himself with it in the deeper waters, doing his fishing with a single hand, but still so masterfully that his handicap was little noticed.

The two men finished their talk and announced to Mark that he would have free rein to do as he pleased, have his choice of the water, and a club warden to go along with him if he liked. They wanted to give the old man the best on this trip, for, as a club affair, this was to be the last fishing at Hazel.

That day and the next, two dry-fly artists—one conventional, the other most *un*conventional—opposites in their manner, tactics, and style, enjoyed two of the best days of their career.

Late on that final afternoon the Captain caught up with Mark, standing on a rock teasing a sizable trout. As he paused to watch the same show he had witnessed many times before, Stikeleather walked up. Mark had seen the trout, and the trout had seen Mark. Mark had missed hooking him on the first rise, and the trout swiftly returned to his place under a near-by rock. The old man was determined to bring him out again. He had taken thousands of trout which had seen him and his flashing rod, and he was going to prove that it could still be done.

The two men stood and witnessed one of old Mark's greatest performances. Mark danced the fly back and forth on the side of the rock where the trout was hiding. The fish was aware of the presence of man, but the fly danced with such cunning the trout just couldn't resist it. He was weakening—two or three times he darted from his rock toward the fly, only to turn back to his hiding-place without taking.

"Just keep watching him, Captin," Mark said. "I'm gonna aggravate him till he'll forget about me; then he'll fasten on."

And he was right. After several darts out and back, the fish finally abandoned all caution and took that fly. As Mark was putting the fish in his basket, the red sun was saying its farewell to the valley of Proctor before sinking below the sharply etched line where the green Smokies met the blue sky. The two men had seen Mark Cathey win his final battle brilliantly and take his last fish—in this world.

Putting the fish in his basket, he stepped to the bank and said: "Well, I'm through, gentlemen." There was much truth to his words. That trout ended Mark's career.

On a crisp morning two months later I picked up the paper from under my office door. Mark Cathey's picture was on the front page. The veteran was dead. The night before, they had found him near midnight at the base of a big hickory, his squirrel rifle across his lap. The manner of his going was altogether fitting—out in the woods he loved so well, in the golden month of October, under the starlit sky.

CHAPTER VII

Other Trout Streams

Although I have touched on a few of the more noted trout waters of the limited Smoky Mountain section, these constitute but a small portion of the streams of equal interest that are spread over the southern Appalachians. These waters are scattered through a belt at least two hundred and fifty miles long and half as wide, so let us drop a fly lightly over some of the best known of these streams.

In the extreme tip end of western North Carolina, six miles northwest of Hayesville, is Fires Creek. It has long been one of the better rainbow streams. Judging by the annual take of several recent seasons, trout coming from this creek average about ten inches. Each season, however, a substantial number of twelve- to sixteen-inch fish are taken, and with favorable conditions Fires Creek seldom fails to give a fair basket. Most of it is in the Fires Creek Refuge and open only at prearranged periods. Shooting Creek in the same locality, fourteen miles east of Hayesville, is a fair rainbow stream, supporting three tributaries that offer both rainbow and brook trout.

In the twenty years I've known the Nantahala River, it has been good rainbow water. There are rough stretches that only the most nimble-footed can negotiate, but flowing through a sparsely settled, rugged country are good lengths of excellent water. Part of it is in the Standing Indian Refuge, and part of it is controlled by a private club, on which fishing is allowed for a fee. The Nantahala has several very interesting tributaries, and rough they are, but the fishing has its rewards.

Toxaway River and White Water River, southwest of Brevard, North Carolina, in the zone of streams that flow across the line into South Carolina, are two most rugged streams that are perhaps fished less in proportion to their trout content than any others in this region. There's a good reason. These two rivers flow down through a country so rough that fishing is a challenge. In the summer of 1946 an experienced angler, a thin wiry man with whom I've fished for years, who relies on these two rivers for many of his trout, took a man of the city in to fish White Water. This man was fat and chubby, and it was his first venture at trout fishing. After a three-mile hike to White Water he was actually frightened at the extreme ruggedness of the country. Late that afternoon the experienced angler returned to where they had first come down to the river, with a magnificent basket of rainbow and speckled trout. His companion, feet still dry, was impatiently waiting. The rushing white water and the clifflike gorges had stopped him right there. He shook his head and said: "No—trout fishing isn't for me. If it's to be this way, I'm through with it for life."

Just below where this stream crosses the North Carolina line and pitches off into South Carolina, 'way down there where, from above, a man looks like a speck on the sand, perhaps a thousand feet down (I don't think it's ever been measured), and where the sun never shines, there is a chain of pools, spacious and deep in their solitary magnificence. They are inhabited by the granddaddies of brown and rainbow trout. Indeed, they are a tempting chain of pools, grand to the last drop and holding rich rewards. Not many North Carolinians have fished them, and few South Carolinians. The almost straight up-and-down cliff, the only way by which they can be reached, is a challenge to the most sure-footed, painstaking angler. The slightest slip would mean a life. But I have known several who negotiated the dead ends to reach the chain, and they brought some grand trout back up the cliff. For obvious reasons it is one spot, I think, where no one worries much about a South Carolina license if he has the nerve to keep on going down. One man who failed to mark his way down was forced to go out through South Carolina. Another had to climb trees to get out; but most trouters, after one long look, decide they haven't lost anything —'way down there.

With little fuss about it and without the knowledge of the angling public, in the years gone by, brown trout were stocked in these grand streams. Of brown, rainbow, and speckled, some of the heaviest creels come from Toxaway and White Water, including a four-pound and a seven-and-one-quarter-pound brown taken during the season of 1946. They are predominantly spinner or wet-fly water, but with only state regulations for streams at large applying, they are also fished with bait. The two large browns mentioned were taken that way, as are most other really big browns and rainbow. For the angler who knows his way about and likes a country far from the bright lights, so rugged and solitary that it is lonely, Toxaway and White Water are like that.

In the Pisgah National Forest, southwest of Asheville, there are several convenient streams where good brook and rainbow fishing is available much of the time. The North Fork of the French Broad River, where the upper waters are governed by special regulations and only state regulations apply to the lower waters, is one of the favored Pisgah streams. Many fine fish have come from this water, including prize-winners, and as the seasons come and go, good fishing is fairly consistent, with both species averaging slightly larger than in other Pisgah streams. In a survey, some years ago, of western North Carolina streams to determine the quantity and character of stream-bed insect life, the North Fork of French Broad rated highest in this respect.

In the lower waters of the North Fork there aren't so many trout, but there are some large ones, and enough of them to be inviting to anglers who like the idea of fishing for a big one. Things haven't always been pleasant, however, for those who went to this lower stretch to try for a big rainbow, including myself, but in due time we have learned.

A short way up from where the fork begins, a man lives, or did live, on a tract of land that skirts the stream for more than a mile. He had little respect for anyone who "toted a fishpole"; in his estimation such people were definitely no good to the country and were just a trifling feather-tossing class that ought to be put to work. When this fellow saw a fisherman up or down stream wading in the direction of "no man's land," he had his say in no uncertain terms and seemed to enjoy being nasty about it, with more than a little profanity added when he felt like it, as he usually did. But a day came, and quite interesting was the climax that came about.

One morning three fishermen were headed for North Fork. Two of them had suffered under the tongue-lashing of this country bully. In the meantime they had learned that he didn't own the land in question, but was a renter, and that the true owner was willing for all to fish. Somewhere on the way up these two decided their companion might serve a good cause. He was big and tough, the kind who can lift the back end of a fisherman's car out of a mud-hole, a good fellow, but one who never backed away from a good fight. As they motored along he was told about the large fish in the lower water of the fork and it was suggested that he might have the first try on this fine water. When he was dropped off on the fork and given instructions to fish upstream a mile or so, where they all would meet, he was also given further instructions. An old house was described and the man living there, a screwy half-wit, who fancied he owned all of North Fork and whose harmless pastime was to annoy fishermen. He was further advised that in case the nitwit came down to the stream, a good blast of cussing would send him on his way. As a final gesture, to pep things up a bit, he was handed a flask. Going on upstream, the plotters began to fear the situation portended danger—but it was too late then. Anyway, it wasn't too bad, for, preceding the fight, here's what happened.

A country man approached the stream swiftly. "Who told you yu' could fish my place? Git the hell out o'ther and be'n a hurry 'bout it."

Two swigs, little needed by this fisherman in an instance like this, were nevertheless taking hold.

"You're telling me? You go to hell; no country mossback like you is telling me what to do."

"Go to hell yerself—I've hadda nuf o' you bug-throwin' fellers. If you ain't out in a couple of jumps you'll be pickin' some shot outer yer carcass."

"Why, you damn hayseed, let's see what the hell you can do about it, if you'll come down here. *Come on down*—I'll bat the hell out'a you and then do my fishing. You don't see me leaving, do you?"

"I'll skin your damn hide fer leather. I'm comin' down, you ——."

"*Come on*—I don't want much excuse to whip a fish-hoggin' bluffer like you."

Besides being drenched in cold water, the bully was soundly thrashed. That put an end to his reign of the North Fork.

Davidson River, a beautiful stream that slips along quietly, is fished more than any other water in the Pisgah zone. There's a hatchery on the stream, and it is stocked frequently and adequately. Some years it leads all refuge streams in number of fish taken, but the size averages slightly less than that of those taken elsewhere. Rainbow trout predominate, but there are some brookies. Davidson has several trouty tributaries; Looking Glass Creek with its beautiful falls, near lower Davidson, is a picturesque little stream that has captured the fancy of many anglers. In Pisgah streams fishing is usually good, but recently it has become somewhat spotty. On South Mills River I've had many exciting battles with rainbow and brown; it is water as well suited to one as the other. Speckled trout are also to be found in the tributaries and head waters of these last three streams.

A worthy rainbow stream that rises on the Mount Mitchell Refuge, forty miles northeast of Asheville, is South Toe River. It has long been fished by the natives and a few visiting anglers, but Neels Creek, a tributary, is much more important and attracts much wider attention. On this creek no men are allowed. It has been set aside exclusively for female anglers, and rather naturally it is kept stocked heavily with legal-size fish. During the warm season, when a minimum of clothing is conducive to comfort, the girls have a great time of it on Neels Creek, and they do take many creels of trout.

Continuing northeast of Mount Mitchell is a belt of good streams covering a strip of country a hundred miles in length. Some of them I've had the opportunity to fish and some I haven't, but it is a country that, in addition to rainbow and brook trout, is better known for its brown-trout waters. Big Wilson Creek, aside from being magnificent bass water (as treated elsewhere), in the opinion of many, including myself, is the best combination trout stream in that part of the country. When bass fishing in the summer of 1946, at a time when trout fishing usually tails off, a mixed basket of ten rainbow and brown—running from fourteen to nineteen inches—convinced me that Big Wilson is still living up to its reputation. I have a fishing friend living near Big Wilson who gives away more trout than any other fisherman I know, and this stream is his standby. Some of his best browns come from the public water below the refuge. Beginning near Linville, North Carolina, it is a stream of substantial length and good tributaries and is a favorite with those who know it best.

Some years ago during the spring trout season it suddenly came over me that I'd never fished Linville River. I had long known the stream was locally famous for its big browns, in addition to rainbows. It is a stream where anglers about the country go to try for one of the monster browns. I decided to drive up there and see if I could get a look at one of the twenty-four- to thirty-inchers that were so frequently reported. On a three-day trip to Linville a survey of several miles of stream that included some fishing revealed it to be typical brown-trout water. However, the trip was a little disappointing. Because of my lack of experience with the big browns, only a few small fish were my lot.

I did, however, *see* what I was looking for—two of them. One was a fish, unseen but suspected, that I tried hard to raise, which upon a too close approach took leave from under a rock in slow water and moved lazily into the pool a hundred feet above. The other brown, measuring close to three feet, had previously been caught by a resident of the Linville settlement and was residing in the pool of the near-by golf-course stream. He had been deceived with live bait just before dark one evening in the run-off below a pool where he was played gently for a long time, then removed to a tub (which had been sent for in the meantime) and transferred to the course pool, where people might see what inhabited the river. When I looked down at him in his pool he seemed to be sleeping. There were several eight- to ten-inch rainbow cruising about the pool, but at a safe distance from the monster.

Linville River begins under the north side of the noted Grandfather Mountain and flows through the mountain settlement of Linville, a high-up, quiet, and beautiful village that is largely a secluded tourist haven during the summer. From there it flows down through the rugged Linville gorge, where trout abound, and then it empties into Lake James.

Another stream of this range long noted for its big trout, rainbow and brown, is Elk River, on which tournaments for big fish were held prior to the war. Still another is Flannery Fork, south of Boone, North Carolina, renowned for its fine rainbow. Also there is Graggs Creek, a soft little stream (except in its upper waters) where I well recall the work of a dry-fly artist a few years ago. One afternoon amid showers I followed and watched while he took a nice basket of fish that were a cross between rainbow and brook. A quaint little stream it is, and throughout this region there are many others like it in one way or another.

CHAPTER VIII

Smallmouth Streams

Good smallmouth-bass streams in the immediate Smoky region aren't too numerous, but there are a few, and, as might be expected in an area of many trout streams, they are underfished. It should be brought out that the bass waters in the park zone are the lower waters of the trout streams previously discussed, in most of which bass overlap the trout for a considerable distance. The smallmouth of the streams average somewhat smaller than those of the lakes, as is to be expected when game fish inhabit both stream and lake in the same region. Stream bass average from one to three pounds, with some four-pounders and an occasional specimen of five pounds, but these unusual stream specimens can be exceptionally difficult to catch when using artificials.

On the Tennessee side of the Smokies, Abrams Creek offers fair bass fishing. From the stream mouth, where it empties into the Little Tennessee River, to Abrams Falls, fifteen miles upstream, is all smallmouth water. However, in the upper stretches, from Abrams Falls about five miles down, rainbow trout overlap with the bass. Another stream on the Tennessee side is the middle prong of the Little Pigeon River. Good bass fishing here is limited to a four-mile stretch, beginning at the park boundary and ending at the Green Briar Cove.

Perhaps the finest smallmouth stream in eastern Tennessee is Little River. For twenty-one miles below the well-known sink holes (which for a long time have been an odd, irregular water-marked area) it is grand bass water. The six miles of water from the boundary up to the sinks is combination bass and rainbow-trout water, but from the boundary fifteen miles down you have only smallmouth. Except for an occasional shoal, up and down this lower stretch wading is difficult, the water being too heavy for a fly-rod man. On the other hand, it is ideal water for the boat fisher, using either fly or casting rod.

On the North Carolina side, smallmouth are native to the lower waters of Eagle and Hazel creeks, which now flow into Fontana Lake. However, trout outnumber bass in the same waters, and they are therefore less attractive to the inveterate basser.

Oconalufty River is without question the best bass stream on the North Carolina side. Like other streams containing bass, for several miles above the park boundary to where the trout take over entirely, it is combination water. Below the boundary—through the Indian reservation and on down—it is a big, fast-moving stream. From the reservation down to a small lake into which it empties, a distance of about ten miles, it is almost exclusively bass water. This stretch is noted for its large pools, all of which hold their share of bass, a few, really big ones. While some of this water is too expansive for the fly-rod, most of it can be waded and reached by this means.

While rated the best bass stream in that locality, it is a stream, I confess, that has defeated me more often than any other, perhaps two out of every three times. Not a good average, by any means. Some of these defeats on Oconalufty can be charged to unfavorable conditions; others to failure to sink the lure deep into the depths of the large pools, where the good bass mostly lie. There have been a few forward casts, however, that didn't come back, and in the future I'm hoping to better the present average.

As is characteristic of large water, this is a stream of large bass. It is fished mostly by bait fishermen, and they can only touch a small portion of its fishable water. It deserves more attention from the fly-rod man than it has received.

Here may I be pardoned for leaving the main stream, so to speak, to tell a true smallmouth story? The "boy-girl" angle is incidental only. Primarily it's the story of the greatest stream thrill of my life, the story of a smallmouth stream.

One day in March came a phone call to know if I would teach a man's daughter how to catch a bass on a fly. The girl, it seemed, was in college up north, but had particularly mentioned my name as her instructor when she got home in June. I put it down as a girlish whim to be forgotten by summer, and thought no more about it.

July came, and the gentleman called again. His daughter was now home, and would I drop by some day and "talk it over"? The following day the girl took things into her own hands and called me— would I do something about it that afternoon?

I drove out to find her waiting impatiently on the ample lawn at the side of their home. Stream fishing, it seemed, was what she had on her mind, stream fishing, but she had no knowledge whatever of fishing; in fact, she had never had a rod in her hands. I recognized much sincerity of purpose in the young face, but had little confidence in the outcome.

There on the green lawn I assembled a rod and attached a dummy fly to the leader. She looked on with interest, but I made no effort to let everything look simple. For the next few minutes I demonstrated the theory of fly-casting, explaining that while it might seem academic on the lawn, she must know the theory to be successful on a stream. She listened patiently, almost despairingly, I thought. As expected, when I handed her the rod she was actually

[65]

afraid of it. With a little coaching she managed to get the fly out a few feet. I impressed upon her that she was taking up a sport in which there was much to learn, and that eight or ten lessons would be needed before she could wade a stream. She should think over for a few days whether she still wanted to go ahead. I had no expectation of hearing any more of it.

The next morning she called and announced that she was anxious to go ahead with the second lesson. When I got to her home, her greeting was: "Why did you try so hard to discourage me yesterday? Were you surprised when I called today?"

Realizing that I might have been a little severe, I saw at once an unyielding determination to master that fly-rod, so we went to work.

At the fourth lesson she could keep thirty feet of line in the air without touching the grass; she was doing well with the accuracy target and shooting a fair amount of line. The lesson over, I suggested that she get a good fly-rod outfit and practice without me. "Oh," she remarked, "I have a rod—it has your name on it—I meant to tell you. I'll go in and get it." I remembered the rod, but not to whom I had given it. Very interesting, I thought. I admired her courage and was determined to give her my best.

At the eighth lesson she could lay the fly in a bicycle tire at forty feet eight times out of ten. Her timing was without fault. She had mastered the side cast and the roll cast and could reach a distance of sixty feet. "You're about ready for the stream," I said. Her answer was a bit revealing. "Oh," she exclaimed, "I must hurry. I'd love that."

At the stream the next afternoon an unexpected casualty left us with a single rod between us. There was nothing to do but make the best of it. With light boots, well hobbed, she was very much at home in the water; wading would be no problem with her. Most of the afternoon was spent in explaining stream technique: the

[66]

most probable water; the quiet approach to a bassy-looking pool or flat stretch; the roll cast across the stream, the side cast under hanging bank growth, even a short steeple cast. Passing from lawn to stream was not all smooth sailing, of course, and bass were coming slow that day, almost not at all. However, she did get a touch of life on the other end; on both occasions it was only a bream, but at least she learned the feel of a fish. Between her own sunnies and two bass that I hooked and let her land, it was a fair beginning.

The next morning there was a knock at my office door. I recognized one of the voices before the door was opened. She had brought Bob, a young lieutenant. I remembered the face of a young man, who two years before, had talked me out of a good rod. He was on furlough and his greeting was: "How soon can we go bass fishing?"

"Tomorrow," I said. "If it's fishing, it's always tomorrow." I smiled and that is how we three, next morning, turned up little Caney Fork, ten miles south of the Smoky Park, as day was breaking.

Two miles up from the bridge where the stream flows into the Tuckaseigee River, we parked and, after rigging our rods, selected separate stretches of water. I chose to go downstream. That morning either the fishing was far from good or else my mind was not on it. I knew every foot of the stream, but up to noon I had only one worth-while fish. When we met for lunch I found Bob had gone one better. Fay, the girl, had felt two strikes, but had failed to get fast to her fish. The boy could fish, and I determined not to be beaten in the afternoon. They wanted to fish for rainbow on one of the upper prongs, so I let them drop me off at a stretch of water that flowed through open country for perhaps a mile. On the lower half of it there were just four fishable pools. As a bass fisherman, I had my reasons for fancying this particular stretch.

In any good smallmouth stream where pools are separated by a substantial distance of fast shallow water (the kind of water where a bass will not stay), you can generally depend on them to hold two, sometimes three good fish. At least I have found such water more certain than a series of pools close together, where perhaps one out of four or five may deliver. Also, in fishing such water a bass fisherman frequently works too fast. I well remembered that the three bass taken on a first visit to this open water the summer before were hooked after upwards of fifteen to twenty casts.

With all this in mind, I began fishing the lower pool, using a green weaver pattern of bucktail with a tiny gold spinner attached. On the third cast to about the center of the pool, I saw the tail of a smallmouth as he turned, under the lure. He must have seen me—nothing was added to the creel.

I stopped well below the tail of the next pool, stripping an extra length of line instead of taking another two or three steps. Nothing happened in the tail water. Up near the head in the deeper water I was attracted, as always, by a milkish-looking spot of bottom water, caused by a small area in which the sand had settled. The experienced stream basser knows just that kind of bassy spot. With two small shot on the leader, the cast was dropped above and to the side so that it would have time to sink by the time it crossed the milky spot. I left that pool with two "keepers" in the basket.

In the third pool a small fish was hooked that ruined any further possibilities there, which left only the upper pool, about two hundred yards upstream. The summer before, I had taken a last bass of the day there, but it wasn't a large one. While playing it, another—the largest I had ever seen in that stream—came out from a rock cave under a huge boulder on the far side and watched the fight of the smaller fish for some seconds before returning to his rock. I had to leave him there, for the very good reason that I couldn't induce him to take. Unless some country lad had snaked him out with bait, he must still be there. For a mile upstream there was no pool he would notice, and the pool below—with which no doubt he was well acquainted—was far less attractive to a fish like him. Certainly I had not fished so long that the thought of such a fish didn't register a thrill.

If still there, he'd be back in the dark water under the boulder. After all, he was the only fish in the pool that mattered. Instead of working all the pool, therefore, I decided to cast directly to where he was most likely to be. Yard by yard—very slowly—I worked up-pool to where, from the tail of a whirling eddy, the water came in fast under the boulder. If he didn't come there, I knew he wouldn't at all. I began sending the lure to the black recess where, in time past, a hunk of boulder had cracked off, allowing the current to cut in under. The casts were good, but not until after twenty or more to this identical spot did it happen.

There was no rush, I hardly felt the strike. There came a dark shadow, the lure faded from sight; he sucked it in and started back under his rock. Five minutes later I was handling him gently in a shallow strip near the run-off. I was thinking of Bob and Fay. I wanted to present that bass to them. I did. That fine smallmouth, remembered for a year, gave me more satisfaction than any other stream fish I've ever caught.

They picked me up at the bridge by the little mountain church, and when Fay saw that bass and heard Bob rave over him, I knew then that my lessons had added a full-time feminine member to the brotherhood. I knew it again when, before the furlough was up, I got a wedding invitation. Little Caney Fork had been very kind. Strange what smallmouth streams can sometimes do!

Far back across the range to the extreme eastern tip of the southern Appalachians, where the mountains gradually give way to rolling country, there are a number of smallmouth streams that are the best in this general region. This conclusion was reached several years ago when I was spending a few days in that part of the country taking census of the smallmouth waters. What impressed me most, I think, was how little the streams are fished in comparison with the fine fishing that awaits one, and how negligible is the use of artificials when compared with the quantity of available water.

Two streams that impressed me much were Big Wilson Creek, which comes down from Linville way and empties into the Catawba River, and Johns River, flowing down through Burke and Caldwell counties a little farther northeast. Johns River is one of those nice softly moving small rivers where the bass population is continuously substantial and where any basser, as well as enjoying the day, will feel much action on the other end. Big Wilson, especially the slower water below the refuge boundary, is typical of its name; it is big water, which for several seasons I've recommended to anglers who wanted to work a stream where big smallmouth are plentiful. Fishing Big Wilson is not at all like working small water in which the whereabouts of bass can easily be determined. While bass, and big ones, are abundant, unless the fisherman takes the stream when they are on feed near the surface, or in the shoals or shallows, he may easily be defeated. That is, unless he knows his bass pools and how to fish them by stringing three or four shot on the leader and going down deep, near the pool bottoms, with his fly—or, even better, a spinner fly. Then Big Wilson will occasionally bring great bends in his rod.

The season of 1946 was a good example of how, for years, we sometimes overlook good water right in our own region. A professor at a boys' school in Caldwell County, North Carolina, George F. Wiese, a gentleman and a finished angler, whose avocation is following the streams, came in to see me. He invited me to come down and fish two smallmouth streams that, except on the map, I'd never seen or heard discussed. They were Buffalo Creek and Elk Creek in the foothills farther east of Big Wilson. I finally went down and looked up the professor. To my disappointment, he was unable to go along, but one of his students who knew the bass waters well took me to Buffalo for the day.

From where we rigged up at the County Bridge, I immediately recognized it as typical smallmouth water. It was one of those slow lazy streams in which, if bass are there at all, they will be found all the way up to where the mountain falls cut them off, or overlapping with trout (as is the case with Buffalo) until an area is reached where the stream temperature falls too low for smallmouth. Starting in at the bridge that morning, I spent four hours on the stream, and felt a little on the spot. My companion, declining to take any of the water above me, even when I insisted, spent most of his time at a polite distance below, observing minutely (I sensed) the quality of my work. However, the bass supplied sufficient action on the other end.

When the day was finished, the stream was found to be just as the professor had described it. By nightfall Buffalo could have given me many more fish, but other things were happening in the meantime. It wasn't all fishing that day. A fall resulted in a cracked rib when I went into deep water for a bass that, with the fly still in his mouth, had wedged himself solidly between two small boulders. The other was a diamondback rattler that my companion failed to kill completely. On our way back a huge black snake had found the injured rattler and was finishing him off. But a nice bass stream indeed is Buffalo Creek, as is Elk Creek, about ten miles beyond.

One morning some years ago a man stopped me on the street and said: "Jim, do you know about New River? It's about a hundred and twenty-five miles northeast of here and flows across the Carolina line into Virginia."

"No," I replied. "What about it?"

"Well, I'm here to tell you, Jim, it's the best bass stream this side of the Rockies."

"Ever fish it?"

"No, but I'm going to! I've been over there, and those countrymen bring in more smallmouth than I ever thought were in this part of the country; and they're big ones—big ones, man—the biggest stream bass you ever saw."

This sounded interesting and, knowing him to be quite a fisherman, I relied on his judgment.

It was a good three hours down to the big concrete bridge that separates North Carolina and Virginia. The water was too soiled for my kind of fishing, there where the river was big and broad, but all up and down, for a long way, bait fishermen on the bank and in boats were taking bass. I retired to a trout stream, but there were other days on this fine river. What more can be said about New River would be little more than what has been said about Big Wilson Creek, except that it's even better. Beginning in North Caroline above Boone, and with good bass tributaries coming in, it grows fast as it meanders toward Virginia. All the way from near the head waters it is a fine bass stream, and perhaps my friend was not too far amiss when he said: "Jim, it's the best stream this side of the Rockies."

❧ PART TWO ❧

Lake Fishing in the Great Smokies

CHAPTER IX

Fontana

Hunger in the midst of plenty is an axiom with which many an angler is familiar, for it is possible to find waters with too many fish and too little fishing.

I remember a day, after fishing the Nantahala, just across the range from Fontana, when three anglers from Kentucky drove up to the landing. They were looking for new water to fish. Having fished lower Fontana for several days and taken limit catches each day, they now sought waters that would be tougher to solve.

Fontana lies in the heart of a mountain wilderness famous in its own right. Before discussing the fish life, I should say something of the lake's geography, size, depth, and dam construction. The man-made wonder of its new dam creates a reservoir thirty miles upstream on the gorgelike Little Tennessee River, extending to the town of Bryson City. Its northern shore is bordered by the Great Smoky Mountains National Park; its southern shore lies within the boundary of the Nantahala National Forest. With its 274-mile perimeter, all heavily forested, Fontana offers an abundance of shoreline for the many varieties of fish native to the main stream and tributaries prior to impoundment. With an area of 10,570 acres and 1,100,000 acre feet of storage, it is the deepest lake in the Smokies. Its dam, stretching 2,330 feet across the gorge of the Little Tennessee, and rising 480 feet from the bottom of the river bed, is the tallest in eastern America. Closure of this dam, which in height and volume of concrete ranks fourth in the world, took place as recently as November 7, 1944—less than three years from the beginning of construction.

Because of its lack of age, one might conclude, in respect to its game fish, that this lake is unworthy of appraisal, but that is not the case. The other older, man-made lakes of the region cannot be used as a criterion for measuring the worth of Fontana, because none of these lakes is fed by such glorious inflowing streams.

The Little Tennessee River, and tributaries which make the lake, is the natural habitat of the smallmouth bass, which from the moment the water reached its present level were found in abundance. This fish is also native in all three secondary streams—namely, the Nantahala River, flowing in from the south, and Hazel Creek and Eagle Creek, emptying in from the north.

The largemouth bass began to show up prominently the second year after impoundment, and at this early date it is highly controversial which of the two members of the tribe will ultimately predominate.

Then there is the rainbow trout. The role to be played by this fish in coming years is decidedly conjectural. At first, fine catches were reported, but, as might be expected, they were confined to definite localities and, as a rule, were made by those who fished solely for trout, anglers who had long known the trout streams that now empty into Fontana. On the north shore of the lake, but widely separated, are four such trout streams. They are Eagle Creek, near the dam end of the lake; Hazel Creek, uplake about ten miles; Forney Creek, about midway of the lake; and Noland Creek, seven miles above Forney. Three of these streams are treated elsewhere in this book. Being fine rainbow streams in their own right, they will undoubtedly continue to be a source of trout supply to Fontana.

One of America's leading ichthyologists, Dr. R. W. Eschmeyer, after a study of Fontana's fish life, contends that Fontana may well develop into a still better rainbow-trout lake. He finds it better suited to trout than any other lake in the mountain region. Several factors contribute to this possibility. First, the streams entering the lake provide excellent spawning grounds. Then, the aquatic food in the lake is adequate and of a variety conducive to trout growth. Finally, Fontana, being very deep, provides a wide variance in water temperature. Thus, depending on season, there is always a depth of water with a temperature favorable to trout. Regarding this depth, something else should be mentioned here. Fontana Dam has no spillway across the top, the water being discharged near the center of the river bed at the bottom. In the interest of fish life this is of real value. In any lake where water is discharged over the dam, a belt of dead or stale water, lacking in oxygen is created at the lake bottom. But with the water drawn from the bottom, as at Fontana Dam, the lower belt of stream-bed water is kept fresh and aerated. This is one of the few lakes in the country discharged in this way.

Regarding other fish, the usual variety of pan fish are there, but they are little sought after. Prior to impoundment of the Little Tennessee, the muskellunge (Esox ohioensis) was native to that stream, one of the two streams in western North Carolina in which they were found. They have been identified as a species inhabiting the Ohio River and its tributaries in several mideastern states. It will be interesting to see what will happen to the musky population impounded in Fontana. So far there is this to report: during the season of 1946, several musky, ranging from small fish to one of twenty pounds, were taken. There is some evidence to support the belief that Fontana is well suited to the culture of this fish. More years must elapse before authentic data are available.

There has been some recent evidence that fast-growing fish do not live as long as their slower-growing relatives. In fish of the same species however, where widely separated geographically, there is frequently quite a spread in their life span. In Southern waters most fish species grow rapidly. In some of the Southern mountain lakes bass two years old will have the same length as that attained in Northern waters in four years. It has been well established that few bass in lakes of this region reach an age beyond six years. In fact, unless the bass are caught before they are five years old, there is little chance of their ever reaching the pan. Like an opossum, of course, an occasional fish will live much longer than average and attain unusual size and weight.

Returning to the quality of fishing at Fontana, other facts may be of interest. Some years ago a conservation official, presumably well versed in fish culture, expressed a belief that smallmouth bass in western Carolina waters could not reach a greater weight than six pounds. During the summer of 1946, little more than a year after Fontana was created, two smallmouth, one weighing eight pounds and three ounces, the other eight pounds were taken from its waters. I personally authenticated these two catches. The world's record smallmouth is fourteen pounds. At least these Carolina bass were grand fish, without question old mossback inhabitants of the river bed from which thousands of their kind have now been dispersed to the shoreline of the new lake.

The number of bass taken from Fontana that year was little short of amazing. In the spring and early summer of its second year, it was not uncommon to see the majority of fishermen unhitching stringers loaded with limits of fat bass. Excepting the hot months of July and August, anyone who could get a lure out did about as well as better fishermen. For that kind of fishing there was but one answer—a superabundance of fish. There at Fontana I was to hear for the first time the expression: "Too much fish, too little fishing!"

But now to give a somewhat humorous twist to this Fontana

fishing and to that indelible first impression left after fishing any new body of water for the first time. On a trip to Lake Hiwassee, our road passed the new Lake Fontana and we decided to look at it and perhaps fish a little. It was about ten o'clock when we stopped on the southern shore where the narrow end of a long prong of water jutted out to the highway. We saw a long string of freshly painted boats, with a small house near by. Some farmer had evidently gone into a new business. As we walked toward the house, a scrubby-looking cross-bred hound signaled our approach. The dark-skinned face of a young Indian appeared against the front window. At the door appeared a small dark-skinned woman—without question, a Cherokee. For two dollars she would rent us a boat for the day. Just then two boats came in, and four enthusiastic fishermen showed us thirty-two fat bass.

About two o'clock we paddled into a small bay where two fishermen were eating lunch. They were yet several bass short of their limits. We heard another boat motoring in our direction. It came into our bay and we were soon in conversation with one of its occupants, a big fellow inclined to monopolize the conversation. He began telling us what a fine lake it was and how 'most any day he could take his limit in twenty minutes. Considering the play of a fish and all, we thought his twenty minutes a little short—but we were to learn.

"A man has to be good," he said, "and has to know how to get 'em," and then after a short pause: "I haven't fished yet today— I'm going across and pick out a few from that bay over yonder. If you fellows are gonna be here awhile, I'll drop back by." We nodded approval.

It wasn't far across this part of the lake, perhaps four hundred yards. In a few minutes there came a whoop that indicated big doings going on over there. There seemed to be much rod play and a lot of water splashes. One of the men in the other boat had been looking across through a pair of binoculars, and we saw a smile come over his face.

"He's got a limit of bass all right," he said. "Move your boat over here and take a look through these." I was soon in focus, and the doings across the way were very plain to see. The fisherman was just lowering a stringer loaded with bass over the side of his boat. It was clear now that when talking to us, he already had his fish. Presently there was another whoop and more splashes. Soon his motor chugged and he was on his way back to us. Coming alongside, he said: "Well, I got 'em. How you fellows doin'?" and with that he pulled from the water his string of bass. At the sight of the fish, the man with the binoculars (taking it all in good spirit, as we all did) said: "My friend, it's remarkable how you caught those so quick—you must really know your stuff. I wish I had some of it."

"Yeh, you gotta know how, to bring 'em in like that," he responded before shoving off again—perhaps to new territory where he could further exploit his great skill. As fishermen come and go, I had never seen a display quite so obvious.

Before leaving Fontana—one concluding remark. In the spring, bass are largely concentrated in shallow water. At this season they seek the warmer water, which is usually the shallow margins of the bays. The most profitable fishing is to be found by working the shallow margins of the bays, and the months recommended as most likely are the latter part of March, April, May, and frequently into June.

Without question the best time to fish this lake, the time when heavy catches are a definite probability, as with most other large lakes in this general region, is in the spring. A recent trip to Fontana may better tell the story of what spring fishing is like, and

Dr. Kelly Bennett rides a boat on Fontana Lake shortly after the impoundment was flooded, ca. 1945. (Image courtesy of Jim Casada)

The old I. K. Stearns place, known as Solola Lodge, in lower Solola Valley on Noland Creek. Prior to the creation of the national park this was a favored haunt of hunters and anglers. (Image courtesy of Jim Casada)

what awaits the fly-caster or plug-caster if this lake be visited in the ideal season.

During the entire month of March 1947 the weather was unseasonably cold and blustery. The chills of winter hung on through the last week of the month, denying fishermen those warm sunny days usually so common about this time of early spring. Preferring to waste no effort at a time when the surface temperature of the water had not yet reached fifty degrees Fahrenheit, a surface condition that keeps bass down deep and off feed, I waited for better days.

In the first week of April the weather changed for the better, and a few days of sunshine would make Fontana just right for either fly or plug fishing. On the morning of the 10th, after a sixty-mile drive to Bryson City, my companion and I turned down the Tuckaseigee River. The lake was down about fifty feet, but rising, and it was necessary to drive down the old Forney Road about three miles before finding a suitable place to put in the boat. We were putting on the motor when two teen-age boys, bait fishing from the stern of a boat tied up close by, attracted my attention. The bow of the boat was beached, but the stern rested in slack water, and they seemed perfectly satisfied with this state of things. As we were ready to motor away, one of the boys, with a crude reed pole, pulled out a bass that looked to be about an eight-inch fish. For a moment his maneuvers were quite interesting. It was plain that he wanted to keep that fish. He seemed to take my obvious glances in his direction as a suggestion that he return the small bass to the water, and going on in his mind, I'm sure, was the probability of being called to account if he didn't. For a few seconds he held the fish, deliberating what to do. Then, satisfied that I was waiting for his decision he turned his back to me and held the little bass for a second on the other side, out of view. A moment later he leaned over the side of the boat and made a gesture as if he was dropping it back in the lake, but instead he dropped it in the bottom of the boat. To satisfy him, we appeared to be deceived and bade him a good day with the fish.

Herman Nichols, my fishing companion of long standing, had two days previously taken a fine catch of mixed bass from Forney's Channel, which was ten miles straight down the lake. Our fast little motor put us there in thirty minutes by the watch. From the Tucka-seigee River Channel of the lake proper, the Forney Channel leads straight back between two mountain ranges for about three quarters of a mile, and the narrow headwaters of this channel afford excellent bass water. Near by, we saw a fish-stringer, heavy with fish, pulled from the water and another bass snapped on. It was evident that the three boat fishers, already there, had had a busy as well as an interesting morning of it. Out to the right of where Forney flowed in, there was a fairly broad area of very interesting shallow, flat water. Herman pointed there, saying that was the place where just two days before he had taken several good bass. All about, the water was spotted with weedy growths with brushy locust clusters sticking up here and there.

While rigging up our rods, feeding fish were constantly in evidence. As I maneuvered the boat about the inviting places, Herman brought to boat several largemouth, three of them entirely acceptable keepers. For this flat-water fishing he used a shallow-running red-and-white plug that had previously served him well. Twice a fighting bass threw his plug, but hardly had this happened than another was on. Indeed, it was fishing at its best.

When my time came to take the rod, I asked Herman to paddle me along the weedy shoreline, out to the right, leading back out into the lake, which, soon after arrival, I had selected as most probable water. There were some rocks among the weeds, but the trashy character of the water extending several yards out from the shore was hardly conducive to the best of fly fishing; I was positive, however, that this water, if worked carefully, would not be lacking in rewards. Beginning with a green weaver fly, tied on a No. 1 salmon hook that a noted Northern angler had sent me to try out on our Southern lakes, I felt that almost anything would take (with bass in their present mood), but I especially wanted to try out this fly. To my pleasure it proved deadly; two largemouth came to boat and three others were returned to the water—all in a space of less than seventy-five yards.

The next fish—just a little farther downshore—was a four-pound smallmouth that played deep and strong for about eight minutes. Not more than seventy-five feet farther down, another smallmouth took. This time the play did not last so long, as I've often found to be the case when the fish is hooked in the lower instead of the upper jaw. I have never taken a brace of smallmouth more nearly identical in size and looks. Their girth, length, and bronze bars separated by the pale yellow were almost exactly alike.

As we fished on down the shore a short way, the bass continued to take freely and vigorously. In a distance of not more than four hundred yards I'd taken all the bass I wanted, equally divided between largemouth and smallmouth, but including one of the largest rock bass ever to come to my fly, which at first sight was mistaken for a smallmouth. With plenty of time on our hands, we decided to rest awhile, and during the rest period I checked the water temperature at several places about the channel, the average being about 58 degrees. According to this reading, fishing was not yet at its best, as it would be between the 60's and 70's, when greater numbers of bass would be on the prowl.

About noon another boat came up to our end of the channel. Its occupants, we learned, were going to fish a strip of the rocky stream-bed just below where Forney Creek came in, for rainbow trout. Bait seemed to be their choice for this early trout fishing. Shortly after midday my companion resumed fishing, with little effort needed to supply what was lacking on his part of the stringer.

The inclusion of this most recent trip to Fontana emphasizes the quality of spring fishing that may be anticipated from mid-March, *when that month is seasonable,* on to about mid-May, or at such times as the surface temperature of the water goes above 75 degrees. And something else: in the spring the hour of the day is a lesser factor—the fish are then more or less disposed to take a lure that comes their way at any time. Of course, good fly fishing and good results with the casting rod are a strong probability all through the summer months, provided the angler is at the right place at the right time, which more often is near dawn or near dusk. But for those midsummer anglers who prefer the convenience of late sleep and a return to the dock at sundown, deep trolling is the most dependable alternative.

I have treated the fishing at Fontana at some length because of the great interest shown in this new reservoir and the plans taking shape to maintain the fine fishing now available.

CHAPTER X

Nantahala

Nantahala, while not a TVA Lake, merits special mention apart from the other lakes of the Smoky region. South of the Smokies, nine miles from the crest of the Nantahala Range, it is cupped in an out-of-the-way mountain valley little traveled by the average day motorist. This lake, about six miles in length, was man-made from the higher gorgelike Nantahala and its tributaries. Its length, however, should not be a measure of its size, for the winding shoreline meanders in many directions, multiplying its channel length several times. It is the highest lake in the southern Appalachians, and for its sheer beauty of landscape and surrounding primeval ruggedness I know no body of water in the South quite its equal. It is a lake of many coves, large and small, with a branchlet or small stream flowing into most of them.

Prior to the summer of 1946 I had not fished this lake, owing to the fact that it was relatively new, then going into its fourth year since completion, and I am never in a hurry to fish new lakes. But during the summer and early fall of 1946 I made three trips to this lake, totaling ten days, for the sole purpose of examining its entire shoreline from the dam to the upper channel of the Nantahala River. On the first trip a companion and I spent two days making a preliminary survey from a motor boat. From near the broad earthen dam we started up a lake enclosed on all sides by a background of heavily timbered mountains. A mile and a half uplake we entered a narrow pass that leaves the broader expanse of the lower lake behind. There the contour of the shoreline began to take on many shapes, and the water looked very fishy. To our right, a long and fairly broad strip of the lake—with many breaks that indicated cove water—extended farther than we could see. At the entrance to this long arm a picturesque little island, covered with dense vegetation and topped with several lonely-looking trees, attracted us. Cruising slowly up the shoreline, crisscrossing occasionally, we found every variety of cover the angler could desire. Grassy shallows were conspicuous here and there; stumpy water and logs, rock ledges, and other underwater cover were abundant.

A mile or more up the lake we passed a long, scrubby ridge that jutted far out into the lake channel. On the uplake side of this ridge the shoreline took on a rainbow shape for a half mile, and many little backwater pockets could be seen. Here we turned left and started to investigate this attractive piece of water. In one of the backwater pockets a boat was anchored. We slowed up to watch one of its two occupants play and net a nice smallmouth, while the other did likewise with a good pan fish. For its entire length this half-circle strip of water sloped gently for a good distance from the shore, offering a most inviting stretch for either the fly- or plug-caster. I wanted to turn back to the point of the ridge and start fishing there, but we had agreed to explore. All along we noted that fish life was abundant. About the inlets to some of the small coves the water was literally blackened with pan fish.

Farther up the lake the general topography of the mountains gave us the course of the Nantahala Channel. From there on, we by-passed the coves, necks, and other side waters, for the time being, and headed directly up the channel. We expected soon to have a view of the Nantahala where it flows in, but the distance was much greater than anticipated. For the first mile the channel was

[86]

broad and deep, with steep rocky banks on both sides; it looked like ideal water for the bait fisher. As we continued, the channel narrowed appreciably, and from the steep mountain ridges on either side, huge snags of dead chestnut, standing solemnly among the oaks and hemlocks, presented quite a rugged picture.

In a broad bend of the channel we came alongside of three other fishermen anchored near the rocky shoreline. They displayed a nice string of smallmouth bass, averaging two to three pounds, taken with live bait. Artificials had served them well in this same water during the early season, but during midsummer they preferred to fish deep with live bait. Indeed, they were doing quite well with their combination of branch minnows and spring lizards.

As we proceeded around the turns of the winding shoreline, we were presented with much interesting water, expecting at each bend to see the flow of this rainbow-trout stream. Finally, as I was wondering how much farther it could be, we turned one more bend—and there, several hundred yards ahead, were the silvery ripples of the Nantahala coming in fast.

Later I learned that this upper channel water is the favorite fishing ground of the native bait fishermen for large rainbow trout. This later was proved to me when I saw two magnificent catches of rainbow taken from this water; one of the catches of nine trout averaged from fourteen to twenty inches in length.

The next day we explored other prongs of the lake, doing a little fishing at times. I had to work diligently to bring three smallmouth bass to boat. With the pan fish, however, it was easier. Everywhere we fished they were taking consistently, and a fair number were of such creditable size as to be worth mentioning.

The third and last day was more or less another day with the bluegills and rock bass. The smallmouth were difficult and it was not hard to understand why. In this, the hottest period of summer, the surface water was too warm to be conducive to shoreline feed-ing. In the coves at depths of ten feet and beyond, fine specimens could be seen mingled among the thousands of small fry, which provided an adequate food supply at the depth and temperature they preferred.

On another trip three weeks later, my companion was Wade Hampton Harley from Florida, who had been fishing the Carolina mountain waters with me for six straight summers. He is a compe-tent fly-rod man, but when the fly-rod does not produce, his alterna-tive is bait.

For this trip he had made plans without my knowledge. I didn't know that he was an authority on catalpa trees and their pestiferous inhabitants, but I was to learn. On our way to the lake he stopped by a catalpa grove on the outskirts of a highway village. Most probably, I assumed, he had previously spotted this grove, for it soon became evident that in some way it was to be associated with the fishing at Nantahala.

"Now, Jim," he said, "we've got work to do; tomorrow I'll show you the finest bluegills in that lake. Can you climb a tree?"

Since climbing trees held no interest for me, I declined. Presently he was unfolding a white sheet, which was an important item of his plans. I wondered what the sheet was for, but soon the question answered itself. Wasting little time in selecting the most promising of the catalpas, he spread the sheet under it. Shortly, we sighted a lad from the village, riding a bicycle down the highway in our di-rection, and for a silver half-dollar he was induced to climb the tree and shake it. While fat worms were being gathered from the sheet and placed along with some green leaves in a burlap bag, there came a crash from the tree. The boy, with one of the brittle limbs tightly clasped in his hands, came tumbling down. "Damn! This is what bait fishing gets a man into," I thought. I was certain we were going to be presented with a liability, but, no worse from the fall, the smiling lad got quickly to his feet.

The next morning we agreed to alternate between his bait and my fly fishing. It was early when I started to work a twin cove where each of the necks was fed by a nice stream. Three small-mouth were taken near the tips of these coves, where the fresh stream water came in. We then cruised to a small rocky cove across the lake, previously selected for bait fishing. This dark little back-water pocket was out of the way of the bright sun. Rocky and full of sunken logs, it was indeed a fishy-looking spot of water. We eased in and anchored. It was not hard to understand how this pan fishing could capture an angler's fancy. The bluegill, augmented by goodly numbers of rock bass and crappie, were so thick that at times it was impossible to see through them. Most of these pan fish were from six to eight inches long, but big ones could also be seen, together with an occasional smallmouth. Never in any fresh-water lake had I looked upon so many thousands of pan fish.

I just sat and watched my companion lower his catalpa worms. At first and until he changed his tactics, it was impossible to get his worm to the bigger fish. The apparently fearless bluegill—of legal size, but not desirable fish—got there first! They would gang up on that morsel of a worm like sparrows on a crust of bread. It was fun, but the large bluegill were too slow, and to take a bass was out of the question. There were various ways, however, to take better bluegill. The boat was moved out to deeper water, where the school of fish thinned out. But the small fry were there too, to take a slow-sinking worm. This was overcome by putting on more lead to take the bait swiftly to the bottom. Then, by switching the worm out to deeper water where it sank quickly, we got results. In a moment his line would move—faster and then faster, straight out, or maybe in a circle. Almost every time it was an adult bluegill, the kind even a bass fisherman is proud to keep. This latter method proved highly effective in taking large pan fish from Nantahala.

In the early fall of this same year, when the water had cooled somewhat, I fished this lake again. At this time the bass rose much better to the artificials. For the fly or casting rod the latter part of March, April, and May are definitely the most productive months. Then in the fall there are periods when the bass will take again. The fly- or bait-caster who knows his tackle and is willing to work diligently about the mouths of the streams (of which there are many), preferably at daylight in the morning or very late in the evening, may be able to take some nice bass during late June, July, and August. But he may be cautioned here that there are dead spots during the hot months and the fishing may be tough. Competent plug-casters tell me that some good fishing is available during the moonlight nights of these hotter months. I have not yet explored this angle, but judging from experience in other lakes at night, it seems decidedly probable.

For the bait fisherman it is a different story. With the lake open throughout the year, this method may be depended upon from March through November, and to a lesser degree during the winter months. Minnows, spring lizards, and worms, in that order, seem to be the most favored baits.

For those wishing to camp out, there are several good locations, at points adjacent to the lake shoreline. Not far from the lake, situated atop a picturesque knoll, there is a country-like inn where excellent accommodations are available. It is operated by Mrs. O. C. Hall, whose post-office address is Kyle, North Carolina.

~§ CHAPTER XI §~

Chatuge

Less than an hour's drive due south of the Smoky Range is Lake Chatuge, another of the great TVA lakes. Astride the border of northern Georgia and western North Carolina, it rightly takes its place among the important bass and pan-fish lakes.

During the summer of 1943, when it had been created little more than a year, a wide acquaintance with fishermen had brought to my office reports of the fine fishing, but there was a reason. Trolling seemed to be the preferred method. Friends from Asheville, where I live, visited Chatuge and returned with limit catches of large- and small-mouth bass. Considering the short time since its creation, one marveled at the size and numbers of fish, and how they all got there. Cherokee Lake, over in eastern Tennessee, and other TVA lakes, including Norris, had been equally productive too, when first opened. The same reason for this applies to all these lakes. Using Chatuge as an example, why was the fish life so abundant immediately upon its creation, and why does it continue to be so?

It is necessary first to take into account the fish life present in reservoir streams *prior* to impoundment—for instance, the Hiwassee River, which forms Lake Chatuge. As in other streams in inaccessible mountain districts, fish were abundant and little disturbed. When the dam is closed and the water rises, fish leave the stream-bed and spread out along the shoreline, while the water reaches its calculated level; bass and other game fish simply will not stay in the deeper water lacking both food and oxygen.

By the time the water reaches its maximum, the entire fish population (fingerlings and adults) of the main stream and its tributaries have now relocated themselves near the new shorelines. Now, in the beginning there were only so many adult fish in the streams, and the question arises: where do we go from there? The answer is, as stated above, that the mountain rivers held a far greater number of adult fish than had been evidenced by the spotty fishing at the relatively few accessible places.

The next question, as to why these mature fish haven't been quickly caught by the greatly increased numbers of fishermen seeking them on the now easily accessible shorelines of the new lakes, and why this lake fishing does not fall off rapidly, can, I think, be answered by the following causes.

The waters of Chatuge backed up and spread over rich grain fields and pasture lands. From this fertile lake bottom great quantities of organic matter quickly develop, and this in turn supports quantities of aquatic food. Food becomes abundant.

Owing to this superabundance of food, a high percentage of young fish grow to legal size in from eight to twelve months and proceed to propagate themselves. Bountiful food is the sole cause for this rapid growth. Moreover, with so rich a supply of food, there is plenty for all, and adult fish are not so cannibalistic—another factor favoring the young fish. While those lakes are relatively too young for one to predict the future confidently, to date there is no sign of a lessening in the fish population.

To be more particular as to Chatuge fishing, personal experiences covering the first four years of its existence may be in order. What intrigued me most during the first year wasn't the reports of fine catches; instead, it was reports that Chatuge was a lake to troll, that with its clean banks and very clear water it was unsuited to fly-rod fishing. That didn't seem to make sense. I wasn't at all convinced that the fly-rod couldn't be just as effective as trolling, particularly if one had the ability to use a long line. A few days before I visited Chatuge the first time, a doctor with whom I had fished for years, a good trout and bass man, had just returned from the lake. He and his companions had made excellent catches. Knowing him to be a good fly fisher, I assumed that he would attempt to disprove this libel against the fly. To my surprise, he did nothing of the kind; he said: "No, the water is too clear and there's too little cover on the edges; trolling is the only way to take 'em."

I could not remember any lake that had been worked earnestly where the fly-rod had failed to take bass at some time or other. Chatuge was more or less of a challenge to my favored way of fishing, and, thoroughly unconvinced, I decided to find out for myself.

It was a hot afternoon in July. With me were two anglers and one fisherman—if I may thus differentiate. The two anglers were seasoned fly-rod men, possessing more than average skill.

We couldn't begin fishing as soon as we expected. Clouds had been making up since noon, and soon a heavy wind accompanied by rain squalls forced us to take shelter at a near-by farmhouse. It was five o'clock before the weather abated and settled to no more than a fine mist of rain. Since the water in the vicinity of the boat landing didn't look attractive, we decided to cruise about in search of better territory.

We located several patches of backwater shallows, and in one of the better-looking patches we saw a break in the water, followed by a circular wave that faded away. I knew what that meant. A few seconds later I saw the dorsal of a bass. He was chasing minnows in water so shallow it would little more than float him. I wondered if he hadn't knocked a few scales off his belly. The water being somewhat trashy, I decided to tie on a surface popper and present it about the open spaces free of debris. The very first cast exploded the myth that fly-rod fishing would be of little profit on Chatuge. A nice largemouth came up immediately for the popper. We decided then and there that this theory that a fly-rod wouldn't take 'em was a myth.

For the next two hours we settled about the shallows, moving slowly from one to another. Fishing carefully in this manner, we had some interesting moments with not very large but good fighting bass. What interested us most was the sense of direction those bass possessed. When they took in the shallow recesses, instantly upon feeling the hook they would make a beeline for the lake proper. So swift were they that they were on the lakeside of the boat before we got them slowed up and stopped. I still remember one strong fish that, when making a break for deep water, passed directly under the boat. For a second I feared for my rod tip, but somehow I saved it.

We left those shallows with a deep sense of satisfaction. While I had few doubts, we had taken bass with floaters, streamer flies, and spinner flies—the fly-rod question had been settled on Chatuge.

To try out the trolling, we rigged up a casting rod and dropped a deep-running cripple-back astern. Sure enough, the plug hadn't been out a minute before a bass had it. In the space of a few hundred yards three more were taken. It was clear why trolling had become so popular.

It was getting late when we sighted our companions in the other boat. They were working a small, shallow grassy nook. We paused to watch the play of three bass they hooked with a bucktail fly. In this clear and very shallow water, bass were feeding all about their boat.

[94]

As we lingered, our attention was drawn to something else. We witnessed a performance quite out of the ordinary, which one could hardly believe unless one saw it take place. A country boy was handily engaging himself along the grassy shoreline of this nook. His first skirmish into less than ankle-deep water was puzzling, but he came up with a fish, and his purpose was clear. We saw this happen twice. In chasing minnows into the grassy edge, a bass would momentarily get stuck in water too shallow to float him. The boy, with uncanny agility, would spring from the bushes and be on top of the fish before it could get into deeper water. Most bass fishers at sometime have seen a bass beach itself, but seldom for the convenience of a boy standing by. The youth was certainly taking advantage of his opportunities.

The fishing the following days was consistently good. Large- and small-mouth bass were taken by all methods with the artificials. Several strips of shoreline were located providing excellent smallmouth fishing in a character of water that I greatly preferred. There were long shoreline hedges of underwater vegetation and bushes that had not been cleared from the lake bottom. Clustered thickly just under the surface, this vegetation was matted with patches of filamentous algæ, thus creating ideal cover. Those smallmouth would shoot straight up from the bottom like an arrow and have the bug before I knew it.

But now for a look at the other side. Disliking misleading impressions, and to prove that any bass lake, though teeming with fish, is not a cinch and can sometimes defeat the angler, I shall bypass the fishing the following two years, though it was uniformly good, and tell of another trip—the most recent to Chatuge.

One night last June there came a call from my good friend Bill Sharpe, of the North Carolina Bureau of News and Advertising.

He wanted me to meet him and his outdoor photographer at Chatuge. They were to make pictures of the lake and were particularly anxious to get action shots of fighting bass.

We met in the little town of Hayesville and, after dinner, made plans for the following day. Several of the townsfolk had gathered, and it was plain that they had wind of this picture-making business and the advertising that might follow. One of them had seen me work a bass lake before when fishing was above par. His comments showed that he was oversold on my wares. It was embarrassing to hear: "Jim can do this, and Jim can do that." To hear him, who had seen me once only when everything was most favorable, I could have been world champion. He spoke of a big bass he'd recently hooked and lost, but he had the big fish spotted; we'd go there in the morning—we'd get him first—he'd show me just where this whale lived, and we'd have action for the photographer. What an optimist! As if it would be no effort at all to drop a lure right in his mouth! I was clearly in for more than I could perform, and while his intentions were of the best, his good-will talk put me on the spot and there was little I could say.

Bill didn't help matters any by coming up with a story of that past master of bass fishing, John Alden Knight, and his highly professional performance on the bass waters of eastern Carolina. When that story was concluded, my job on the morrow was a far from enviable one.

Although Chatuge was an excellent bass lake, there were ample grounds for my apprehensions. I'd fished for bass too long; I recalled a previous occasion when a photographic party expended two whole days and much film to get a single shot of a jumping bass. And there, with mighty preparations in the making and with only one day allotted for many pictures, and with this fellow pointing me out as the man who could do his stuff, it was fast developing into a command performance. It was an instance where the defense had little chance. There was nothing for it but to wait till morning and do my best. It was one time I would have been pleased to withdraw in favor of a formidable pinch-hitter.

When the loose talk of all that would happen the next day had lapsed into the practical, I remarked: "Gentlemen, I'll help all I can, but don't expect too much. Frequently when the maximum is expected, the minimum results." Bill's understanding nod gave me the satisfaction of knowing that he had been taking the dosage lightly.

The morning was no good for photography when we arrived at the lake. Clouds in every direction dulled the beauty of the mountainous background, but it did look like a good day for bass. While the motors were being clamped to the two boats, and other paraphernalia, including a Speed Graphic, were being readied, I assembled a stiff nine-foot bass rod, one adaptable to extra distance when shallows are to be fished. After some scrutiny of the orange and white forked tailed streamer tied onto a seven-foot tapered leader, we got in and made ready to leave for the selected fishing grounds.

We found, however, that all was not going to be as smooth as anticipated. We had cruised no more than a hundred yards into the lake when the motor on the photographer's boat stalled. For the next hour many manful efforts were made to revive it without avail. Finally we returned to shore and sent one of our party back to town for another outboard. An hour passed, and the occasional rise of a bass could be seen. I felt confident they would take if I could have been fishing just then. A sifted-like mist of rain was now in the air—a mist that frequently enhances lake fishing. While not normally lending myself to fancy notions, I thought right there of Bill's four-hundred-mile trip to get action photos on Chatuge, and I would have been willing, could it have been, for many future ventures to be failures if only this one day should succeed.

Not until midday were we ready to start again. On our way light rain began to fall. By the time we reached the fishing water, a heavy downpour was in progress. Trying to take shelter under the trees along the bank, we got a good soaking from their drippings, and another hour passed. Eventually the skies partially brightened; hopes rose that the afternoon might provide better weather for our purposes. Shortly we were occupied with the business of our task. The photographer's boat was following, camera poised for the anticipated strikes and the ensuing play of the fish. What eventuated during the rest of the afternoon can be summed up in one word.

I have never fished quite so hard in all my life and accomplished less. The afternoon developed into an ideal one to fish; the sun spotted through now and then, the air felt just right, there was a constant soft ripple to break the surface of the water, but not a single bass rose. Floating bugs were offered; streamers, bucktails with spinners attached, were fished just under, then at medium depths and 'way down—ten, twelve, and fifteen feet as a final resort. My companion applied the casting rod, using floating cripples, medium and deep runners; but at no time was there life at the other end. Rising fish had been plentiful during the morning, but after the rain they were completely indisposed to anything offered. Instances like this incline one to believe that even where food is plentiful there may be more significance than many suspect in the sol-lunar theory, a theory that I have questioned where food is scarce and where the fish are consequently keenly on the lookout for tasty morsels. It is for the single purpose of showing how tough a better bass lake can be and that the best-laid plans go wrong that this story is related.

But for the angler with two or three days to spend at Chatuge, the odds are strongly in favor of good fishing. As is common with other mountain lakes, in comparison with its length of thirteen miles Chatuge has one hundred and thirty-two miles of shoreline and covers an area of 7,150 acres. Pan fish are abundant, but of more importance are the two great members of the tribe, the large- and small-mouth bass, which at this writing seem about equally available.

CHAPTER XII

Hiwassee

Although scenic beauty is not essential to the average bass fisherman, who prefers being so busy taking fish that he has no time to look up, it is a desirable feature if coupled with good fishing. Some fifty miles southwest of the Smokies lies a lake that will gratify both the æsthetic and the sporting desires of the angler.

Hiwassee is another of the TVA lakes that came into being through dam construction. For twenty-two miles the Hiwassee River has been changed from a fluctuating stream of little potential worth to a blue lake impounded behind a 1,287-foot dam. As expected, when the water reached its newly created level behind this dam, the fishing immediately became good. It had been openly predicted that after two or three years this good fishing would decline, and that in time Hiwassee would be just another lake. These predictions were based on experience with small power reservoirs in the region, which were providing little in the way of recreation for the angler. The prediction has not come true, however, with Hiwassee.

In the preceding chapter the whys and wherefores of abundant fish life during the early years of Lake Chatuge's existence were discussed. For those wishing to visit these lakes in future years, the findings of qualified fish culturists, based on a longer-range point of view, may well be given here.

Much valuable information has been collected on the fishing potentialties of these larger artificial impoundments. Over a period of years, preimpoundment observations had been made to determine the effect of the change from river bed to reservoir habitat. After impoundment, surveys of the extent, size, and distribution of fish populations were made, together with studies of life span, rate of growth, food supply, spawning habits, and adaptation to the new shoreline environments. Periodically, counts of fishermen were made to determine the extent and effect of increased fishing. Some interesting facts were brought to light. For instance, they disproved the belief, shared by many, that the reservoirs were gradually becoming aquatic deserts, devoid of their original fish life. Contrary to common belief, the evidence disclosed that artificial stocking of game fish in these larger lakes is actually of negative value. It further revealed that so high is the natural mortality of game fish that only a small percentage of the fish crop was being taken by sport fishermen.

These findings resulted in a change of policy. One important change was the decision to open the lakes to year-round fishing. A prominent ichthyologist contended that the closed spring season was not only unnecessary but positively undesirable. Conservation officials were inclined to concede that the greatly increased fish population was not being adequately utilized. On a trial basis only, a lake was selected for which an experimental spring open season was allowed; fishing was permitted during the months of April and May, ordinarily closed for spawning purposes. A carefully taken creel census during this period revealed that 270,000 pounds of fish averaging better than two pounds were taken; yet even this unusually heavy catch had no appreciable effect on the fishing during the remainder of the year as compared with catches of previous years.

Of greater importance, however, was the effect of the year-round fishing in succeeding years. Although this catch more than doubled the best catch in previous years, it was repeated the following year, and again the third year; subsequent examinations reveal no reduction in game fish. There is still no indication that the fish population is in danger.

Also of significance is the fact that adult fish such as the largemouth bass which have passed their reproductive span of life and which are then inclined to feed on their offspring are taken more easily in the spring. Realizing that the latent fish resources were so much greater than were being utilized, the Conservation Commissions of North Carolina and Tennessee have abandoned the closed spring season on the larger lakes. Throughout all the eight years of its existence, Hiwassee has consistently yielded a fine crop of game fish. Notwithstanding the annual winter draw-down for flood control, large- and small-mouth bass, walleyed pike, and pan fish continue to spawn and reproduce successfully. Another factor of interest is the rapid growth of fish. Conclusive evidence supports this, for in recent years large specimens from the new TVA lakes have regularly won regional top prizes. When fishing the TVA lakes of the Smoky region, the visiting angler need not, therefore, fear that his offerings will go wasted on a so-called "fished-out" lake.

But now, to depart from this more or less statistical treatment, let us return to the somewhat lighter discussion of Hiwassee and the character of its fishing from the beginning through to the present time. Near the 1st of March 1946 I received a letter from a man in one of the larger cities of Ohio. It was just one of the many letters received annually through the sportsman's information service of the local Chamber of Commerce. This man wrote for himself and three companions who wanted to spend their vacation near the Smokies. The letter was more solicitous than the usual run-of-the-mill sort asking for information. It at once inspired one to help a fellow get the most out of his short vacation. It rather put me on the spot, since anglers coming to a strange part of the country naturally look to one who is native to his waters with a strong sense of reliability—and rightly so.

Feeling a heavy sense of responsibility, I recommended Hiwassee and suggested April as a most logical month for the best sport. Many present-day fishermen are moon-conscious, so I checked the calendar to give them any advantages the dark of the moon might hold, and advised the middle of the month. In addition to bass, the walleyed pike should be leaving the deeps to prowl about the surface waters about that time. Further suggestions were made regarding tackle and a full supply of lures for both surface and deep fishing. At the designated time the party arrived at Murphy, North Carolina, the town where Hiwassee begins.

I was highly pleased some weeks later when a report of this venture reached me. Everything had materialized favorably. Throughout the days of their stay the fish were taking vigorously. True to their springtime characteristics to be on the move, the largemouth, smallmouth, and walleyes were plentiful along both deep and shallow shorelines. They were favored with bright sunny weather, which is especially desirable in the early months of spring. In fact, the weather was so delightful that for two days they gave up their rooms in town to make camp at a remote spot down the lake. So pleased were they that they made reservations for the following year. While this particular trip was carefully planned, an angler who knows fishing and is properly equipped can find good fishing throughout the season.

In contrast to the above was the experience of two men who visited Hiwassee in August of this same year. They came seeking information about lake fishing, bass and "big bass" were their objective. They seemed to be confused—not about their purpose, but about bass fishing as a whole. They told of recent successes in fishing the coastal waters and how they pulled them in from the ocean's blue deeps. Bass lakes were discussed and they decided on Hiwassee.

Two days later they returned, completely disillusioned. I was not surprised when they complained they had not hooked a fish. They had motored to the lake with little thought about the time of day or proper methods and began fishing about high noon. After hours of happy-go-lucky, hit-or-miss casting, with an assortment of poor tackle, they abandoned the effort. They thought bass fishing in a mountain lake was the same as fishing in the ocean!

Occasionally one comes across fishermen more successful than the average, who are given credit for having mysterious methods or of being casters possessed of uncanny skill; and they do have something. A group of anglers from the state of Georgia had been fishing at Hiwassee year after year and had gained the reputation of being the most consistent bass-takers on the lake. They never failed, by one means or another, to come from the lake with something on the profit side. The manager of the hotel where they put up verified all this. I was inclined to be dubious. Recently, however, I made the acquaintance of one of these men, learned their methods of fishing, and found there was sound basis for their consistent success. During the spring months their methods were entirely conventional. They were good fly- and plug-casters, and they applied both the short and the long rod during the season when such methods were profitable. But when hot weather set in and the artificials failed to produce, bait was the alternative. At such times they worked the deep rocky points where bass and pike had congregated in water that was cool and more to their liking. When this failed too, they had still another alternative. With either live or dead minnows—it made little difference—a unique method of trolling was employed by which they could usually take fish when all else failed.

There was nothing complicated or mysterious about this trolling maneuver, but it was just a little different from the usual. As related to me, two rods were fished from the same boat. With a good length of leader, their hooks were baited with a minnow, dead or alive. The quiet, deep shady banks were preferred. Moving along slowly in this character of water, they fished at different depths and different distances from the boat. While the tailing bait would be weighted to go down deep, the front bait was leaded to travel at medium depth. They didn't depend on the boat merely to pull the minnows along in a lifeless fashion. Instead, they put rod action into play, bringing the minnows near the surface with a series of retrieves and alternate stops, then letting them go down and back up again in the same way. It was similar to the deep fly or spinner retrieving done in fishing straight to the bank from a boat instead of lengthwise of the shoreline. They got results and proved that there are many ways to take game fish from a lake; and so they came by the name "that Georgia bunch."

Although enough has been said about seasonal fishing, any new angle that favors the fisherman instead of the fish is worthy of mention. While too little thought is given to water temperature, it has definitely been established that the depths at which adult bass and pike repose in physical quiet are, with two exceptions, controlled by water temperature. The two exceptions are when the fish go on feed where food is abundant in water in which they will stay only long enough to fill up; and, second, when, after spawning, they linger for a short time with their offspring about the warmer shoreline water. Investigations in TVA lakes have been made recently to determine the approximate depths at which the fish repose. It was found that after the spring foray along the shoreline had reached its peak (when water temperature was just right, between 60 and 70 degrees Fahrenheit), the fish moved into deeper water. As spring progressed into summer, with the surface water warming gradually to 75 degrees Fahrenheit and above, the fish also gradually moved to a still lower belt of water that registered between 60 and 65 degrees. By placing thermometers in the various belts of water where the nets were set, the temperature recordings at a depth in line where the fish were taken established definitely that the fish preferred water near this temperature. There is thus a close tie-in between water temperature and the depth at which bass and pike rest, the pike always resting in deeper water than bass. As a consequence, a table was printed, showing the depth to fish during certain seasons. This table is probably of more value to the bait fisher than to those using artificials. These studies were made not only for the purpose of learning more about fish habits, but in the interest of hot-weather fishing as well. In future years it will not be surprising to see printed tables covering the depths of water where fish are most likely to be found in hot weather. This may seem a bit theoretical, but the facts speak for themselves.

I have fished much in Hiwassee, with many good days and some not so good. I have never seen it crowded with fishermen. Its twenty-two miles of length has a shoreline of one hundred and eighty miles, with many prongs and remote sections. One may fish two or three hours without seeing a boat, and then one welcomes the passing sociability and perhaps information as to what fish are taking. Aside from Nantahala, there is no lake in the Smoky region more beautiful.

CHAPTER XIII

Santeetlah

For some reason Lake Santeetlah is often passed up even by local fishermen for the more favored lakes of the same region, and the excuse most often given is that their stringers will show greater weight for equal effort expended elsewhere. While there may be little question as to the truth of this contention, nevertheless Santeetlah has too many virtues not to be included in the chain of lakes surrounding the Smokies. Some have this and some have that to offer; but each lake has an individual something, and that can definitely be said of Santeetlah. Regarding any man-made lake of age (and Santeetlah has several decades of that) one frequently hears fishermen say: "That old lake is no good any more." Santeetlah is an example of just such sayings. Talk like this should be taken lightly; it may well be that of disgruntled fishermen. While partially true of some of the other lakes, which are to some extent barren of food supply, Santeetlah is not such a lake.

Observation over the years, which includes not only my own experience but the annual reports of others who have fished it diligently, completely confirms its worth to the vacationing angler. Why some find this lake difficult and are defeated more often than not is because it is almost exclusively a smallmouth bass and rainbow-trout lake, the bass taking precedence by a wide margin. And unless I am mistaken, any large smallmouth lake is more difficult to solve from spring through fall than one containing both species of bass. Smallmouth do not give themselves so freely to the hook, and, particularly in lake waters, they are less consistent takers than the largemouth. For years there is this tale said of Santeetlah: most fishermen going there have either nothing to report or a fine catch; rarely does one hear reports of fair success, or that the fishing was just so—it is usually a hit or a miss.

Some years ago, during the month of June, I was asked by another fisherman to go with him out to Santeetlah. I agreed, and the next morning we were on our way. As it was a hundred-mile trip, we left Asheville at something after two a.m. so that we might enjoy a full day on the lake. It was just breaking day when we arrived at the little mountain town of Robbinsville. At that early hour there's not much astir about this sparse little county-seat community, but on a side street we saw a small frame building lighted up, with a sign in front that read: "Meals." On the inside we found it one of those incurious small-town eating-places, with a man and apparently his wife ready to serve us. Unconcerned with the indiscriminate appointments of the place, we sat down at a table where three other men had just finished breakfast. The remains on their plates showed that they had been eating a breakfast composed largely of fish. Without question the word "menu" would have been strange language to the keeper, dressed as he was in overalls that bagged at the knees where his careless leggings began. "You men like a fish breakfast? Got some good fish 'smornin'," he said.

"What kind of fish do you have, my friend?"

"Bass or trout," he replied, "fresh littlemouth or rainbow trout—either one. Bass breakfast's thirty cents; trout'll be thirty-five."

Over behind the counter, where a few packages of potato chips and other miscellaneous knick-knacks were stacked, the woman had her ear tuned in our direction, waiting, I presumed, to put our choice of fish in the pan. On isolated occasions I had eaten fish for breakfast, but it wasn't my preferred morning diet. Here, however, it would clearly be more to his pleasure or perhaps convenience if we ordered fish, and without further ado we obliged. In a moment we heard the sizzle on each turn of the fish, and when the sound of fat in the pan simmered low and faded to nothing, we knew that breakfast was about ready.

When the well-filled plates were brought in, I inquired where the fish came from. "We ketch 'em in Santeetlah—one or two of us here 'n th' fambly fishes the lake, and when we get more'n we need, we fry 'em fer the customers," he told us.

Presently, after the conversation had grown more familiar, he brought out a picture of a string of trout—it looked to be about four or five legal limits—that one of his close acquaintances had taken. But upon further questioning about the fish we were eating, and particularly when asked directly if they were served there regularly, he showed little disposition to be pressed on the subject. As we were ready to leave, two other men came in. The proprietor waited until we were on our way out before offering to serve them. But as I passed through the door the movement of his lips read: "You men like a fish breakfas'?"

After a short drive we arrived at a boat-dock situated on one of the highway prongs of the lake. This was back in the days when I was overanxious to get out on the lake and start fishing as quickly as possible—an ambition that through the years I have learned has gained me little. At that time much of Santeetlah's water was strange to me. But as is the way of fishermen, I had a strong feeling that we were going to have a successful day. Searching for water undisturbed by man, we motored out of the prong and turned down the lake. We were not long in locating a large neck of water that suited our fancy. My companion, first to take up the rod, started casting to a weedy strip of shoreline that shallowed gradually, just right from a fisherman's point of view. Right away he hooked into a smallmouth—then another—but they were both returned to the lake. At that time twelve inches was the minimum length allowed, and while these were legal fish, but with not much to spare, they were returned on the presumption that much better fish would replace them. The morning's activities had started off at such a pace—we were puffed up with optimism—that the day ahead was visioned through rose-colored glasses.

It will take little space to report what eventuated on the lake throughout the remainder of the day—at least, as far as we were concerned. We worked quite a number of strips of beautiful shoreline, beautiful in respect to potential smallmouth habitats; strips of rocky shoreline with those inky spots among the rocks; receding pockets and trashy backwaters; cove waters nubbed with the debris of submerged pine tops—all this netted us a single bass of about three pounds. When we started for the dock in the late afternoon, we little knew that we were to learn that this had been a highly successful day for others.

We were tying up at the dock just a few minutes before dark when another boat pulled in. After laying out their tackle, one of its two occupants pulled from the water a net sack of flapping fish. Through the coarse net of the sack a grand catch of smallmouth was revealed, among them the pink stripe of a magnificent rainbow trout. I hazarded a guess that the bag of fish would reach near fifty pounds. With a few impromptu remarks, not relative to their fish, these men were on their way, declining any discussion of the whereabouts of their fishing or their methods. Several other fishermen came in empty-handed, but we knew that there were some who knew where and how to catch fish.

Back in Robbinsville that night, we found it convenient to park near the place where we had eaten breakfast. We were not necessarily going to have dinner there, but just then we saw inside one of the men of the party that had made the remarkable catch of fish. Somewhat curious, we strolled in and took a seat. The man who had waited on us in the morning recognized us and, walking over, suggested he still had some good fresh bass left if we would like them for dinner. We were certainly not doing so well at catching them, but we seemed destined to have them served to us. On his way to the kitchen the successful fisherman followed him, and, alert to what was going on, I heard the words: "You say forty-seven pounds?" Quite obviously, then, these two men were in collusion in the fishing business. When we came to pay the bill no one was there to take the money, but I heard men talking on the other side of a door that led to the small back porch of the establishment. Under pretense of seeking the owner, I walked over and pushed aside a screen door that I still remember was hanging carelessly from one hinge. Out there in the semidarkness the two were squatted over as fine an assortment of scalloped smallmouth as one would wish to catch. They were easily identified by the beautiful rainbow of at least twenty inches the long way.

Knocking about the little town that night as sleepless fishermen frequently do, I dropped back into the place that made a specialty of fish dinners—and for a purpose. Business was slack and I motioned to the owner to come over and sit down. I explained that we were just visiting fishermen and that he wouldn't be seeing us more than once or twice a year. With a few other preliminary gestures of friendship on my part, we soon arrived at common ground and he opened up. I learned how and where the bass were taken and also that this was not an unusual or infrequent catch for these men. Their method was simple—nothing mysterious at all about it aside from where the scissors were applied! It was related to me as follows:

They would go to a familiar spot where small bream were numerous. By means of bread and a dip-net they got their bait, preferably bream about three inches in length. They fished at the mouths of four incoming streams, Big and Little Snowbird Creeks, Big and Little Santeetlah. The deep clear water covering the boulders where Big Santeetlah poured in was the number-one bet. First a pair of scissors was used to trim off closely the spiny dorsal of the bream. There were two good reasons for this: First, a young bream —for a little while—was much more active in water when thus wounded by trimming the dorsal and constitued a real true-to-life injured minnow. Second, the smallmouth would take them more readily when this sawlike spiny fin was pared—that was the second claim—but put together they amounted to about the same with me. Nevertheless, these fellows knew something about catching bass.

To go now to a subsequent trip where there were four in our party, I remember that first night when I told the boys this story— it was in a cabin by the lakeside where we were putting up for a few days. I had hardly finished when two of our party planned to adopt the same tactics the following morning, and the dial on the alarm was set at four a.m. As usual, I planned to occupy myself with the fly-rod and artificials.

The following afternoon I learned of their success at the mouth of Big Santeetlah. They came to dock, not with limit catches, but with seven fine smallmouth of a size and plumpness that one truly appreciates. They made a much better showing than their two companions. With a knife they had removed the dorsal fin from the bream. That made all the difference. They found it best to fish without a cork, but with a shotted leader to take the wounded bream down deep—ten, fifteen, or twenty feet—to scurry around near the rocky bottom, where the better fish had been located.

From personal experience and the reports of others I can disclose that near the mouths of the four streams mentioned, fishing is consistently good and many fine specimens of rainbow are taken along with the bass. I do not mean to imply that big trout are or can be picked up every day. But they do come to net frequently, unexpectedly, when one is bait-fishing for bass. Nor do I mean to give the impression that the brand of fishing just discussed is all that is worth while at Santeetlah—not at all. Much of its shoreline offers good fishing to the fly- or plug-caster, and many fine catches come to boat in this way.

To pause briefly in the interest of fly fishing at Santeetlah, I well remember a rare experience when fishing the lake with a friend from the eastern part of the state. It was a three-day trip. On the morning of the second day we decided to explore the distant reaches at the lake's western extremity. Whether or not the bass co-operated, we planned to fish hard throughout the day and apply our skill to the fullest. Neither of us had the least idea of the turn of events that the day was to bring forth, or that we were to be rewarded with an unusual experience. After a two-mile run uplake we arrived in the general vicinity of the fishing grounds. A bright morning sun had crossed the rim of the mountains, and, with not the slightest breeze, all indications pointed to a blistering hot day on the glassy Santeetlah. For that reason and because we had missed the opportunity of the early dawn fishing we looked upon the hours ahead with much misgiving. Before us lay a beautiful stretch of shoreline copiously decorated with underwater rocks and the brushy tops of fallen bank trees, mostly pines. Overhanging banks furnished spots of shaded water where a bass might linger for a late morning angler, I thought. In fact, the long shoreline was so attractive that one could find pleasure in casting to it whether or not bass were there.

About twelve o'clock we stopped temporarily for drinks and sandwiches. For three hours we had worked this fine-looking shore, and the shooting of our lures to those likely places had brought forth nothing but an occasional bluegill. We were lunching in the shade on a point, discussing the possibilities of the afternoon. On above us the geography of the shoreline was more broken and rugged—very good-looking water indeed. However, we decided just to rest awhile and await the turn of events, since the sky was thickening up and a change of weather seemed possible. Thirty minutes later heavy clouds began to form and presently the distant rumble of thunder could be heard. A few minutes later rain was falling, but not to our discomfort, because of the warmth and stickiness of the day. When the rain began tailing off about a half-hour later, we resumed fishing.

Suddenly we observed fish breaking water up and down the shoreline. A short distance above the point where we had stopped during the rain, there lay a covelike bay, which extended back into something like a half-circle from the main shoreline. It was perhaps a hundred and fifty yards deep and three hundred yards across. Walking up the shore a few yards to get a good look at this piece of water, I was reminded of a new ground clearing before the brush piles are burned. There was an abundance of cover all the way across this shallow water; lots of fallen tree laps were sticking up over the place; also stumps and an occasional snag. What was more gratifying, however, I could see the roll and break of fish all the way across the place, and these rolls and breaks clearly indicated bass.

We pushed up to this bay and made ready for serious casting. I never will forget my particular feeling as we moved in. It seemed perfect for the kill. A few drops were still falling, and the sky was dark and overcast. There was a gentle breeze and, all in all, within the hour conditions had developed that were typically ideal to bring the basses into action. To add to our anticipation, the water was beginning to boil and fade away in the shape of a circular wave here and there, indicating active fish going on feed. I felt certain our hour had arrived.

It looked like the sporadic feeding spree that bass go on occasionally in hot weather when atmospheric conditions are just right—a spree that the experienced angler recognizes at once and doesn't expect to see more than once a year perhaps, a very different performance from the ordinary morning and evening activities of feeding fish.

While the boat was eased round the bend and I was getting line into the air, a half-sunken pine-top extending from its fallen trunk on the shore some twenty feet out into the lake was selected for the first try. At that instant a roll out in the open water about forty feet to the right caught my attention. I presented there instead and was rewarded with a healthy strike, which some minutes later netted me a smallmouth of about two and a half pounds. The next cast to the pine-top brought up another good one, but on the first run in under his cafeteria he was off. I worked on across the three-hundred-yard stretch to the opposite point, netting only three bass out of about a dozen strikes. My companion couldn't understand it, nor could I. I could not recall any previous occasion when opportunity was so favorable and I was unable to hook not more than every third or fourth fish.

"There's no reason you shouldn't finish out your limit right here in this bay," he said. And there wasn't, for right there in that gentle sprinkle of rain the bass continued to break furiously. Fishing back across to the starting-point, I added four more bass to the stringer, but lost five in doing so. At the moment neither of us could understand why so many bass were tearing loose from the hook. We were to learn.

At this point I insisted on taking the paddle. On the third cast my friend was into a fine one. It was turning out to be a great day and a great trip. In perhaps forty minutes we reached the opposite side of the little bay, and as we finished he hooked and boated his eighth smallmouth in that short space of time. Moreover, he took his limit without making more than forty to fifty casts. Two or three times after he boated his fish, another was on the first time his lure went out.

One more bass was needed to complete my limit. Another sunken tree, with part of its top resting above the water line was selected as a likely place for the final effort. We moved within casting distance and on the first shot to the brushy top brought up a bass. He was on, but after the first run he was off. Something was all wrong. Too many fish were being lost. More bass had thrown the hook during that afternoon than ever before in my entire angling experience. And then something registered with me. All the fish had apparently been hooked very softly, and with several the hook had dropped from their mouths while lifting them into the boat.

The fact that the hook was dressed very heavily with bucktail and the fast and exciting action of the fish had made me forget that I had been fishing with a hook the barb of which had been pressed in to the point where it was little more than a barbless hook.

Some weeks previous I had mashed down the barb of this hook when taking bass from a private pond, bass that were to be placed in another body of water and were to be injured as little as possible.

Never having taken a limit catch on a hook so nearly barbless, I was determined to complete my limit with this same hook. Quite appreciating the handicap, I again presented the bucktail to the source of the last strike, and a few minutes later we had our sixteen fine smallmouth.

The storm and accompanying change in weather had put every

bass in the lake on feed, or so it seemed. It was just one of those wild infrequent, midday feeding sprees which a bass man so longs for. Appropriately and thankfully we called it a day and headed for camp.

That we returned to the same spot of water the following morning can quite naturally be understood. We covered it most carefully, but by midmorning we had boated only one bass. Clearly, yesterday had been our great day. Such is bass fishing!

CHAPTER XIV

Other Lakes

In May 1944 I learned of the new lake over in Tennessee to be opened for fishing on the 1st of June. Since this new body of water, known as Lake Douglas, was created on the lower French Broad River, a stream on which for many years I had fished the upper trout and bass waters, I was anxious to see what it was like.

On the 1st of June three other anglers and I were fishing another lake in Tennessee, but on the morning of the 2nd we decided to have a look at Lake Douglas. I well remember when we first came into sight of this lake, situated twenty miles northeast of the Smoky Range, where the mountains give way to a hilly rolling country.

The sight of its eastern shoreline gave us only a glimpse of its vast area. A drive of two miles along a country road kept us in close contact with the winding shoreline, and we turned to a pasture-like by-road, which led us directly to a broad elbow of water a quarter of a mile away. While making a preliminary survey of the shoreline, a narrow neck of water up to the right, jutting back from the large elbow of water for about a hundred yards, caught my attention. At the extreme point of the neck a cow had come down from a pasture above. Just as she stepped into the edge of water and lowered her head to drink, I saw a wave start sharply a few feet beyond her nose and continue fast, in a beeline, for some distance straight out the cove. It was the telltale sign of a frightened fish. While we had planned to do our fishing from boats that had been reserved on another part of the lake, I made haste to the car for my rod. Another of our party did likewise.

A few minutes later I was ready to cast to the neck. The upper half of the backwater strip looked very "fishy," with much underwater vegetation, and at no point more than eighty feet across. By keeping the line high to avoid a scrubby hill that sloped sharply down to the water's edge for the entire length of the neck, all likely spots of water could be reached from my side. On the first cast a largemouth took, but a moment later he was entangled in a mass of underwater grass. One of my companions, by taking hold of the line near the leader, carefully worked the fish, and almost an armful of grass that surrounded him, to the bank. About that time another bass that had risen to a plug was putting up a good fight down near the mouth of the neck that I had purposely by-passed. Another minute, and another strong fish was heading lakeward with my bucktail.

A third member of the party, a bit slow to catch on at first, could stand it no longer and was making tracks back to the car for his rod. Shortly he was ready for action, but instead of crowding lines in this first little strip of side water, he went around and on beyond to another neck where he would have things to himself. In not more than half an hour he returned with four good bass. In the meantime action had been continuous in the neck where I was fishing. When we gathered at the car, there was an accumulation of fourteen bass. Like the two others, I had retired before reaching the daily bag. We didn't want to call it a day at so early an hour. It was indeed an unusual bit of fishing for just a casual stop by the lakeside. I wondered if that could really be a fair sample of the fishing at Douglas. Truly, it was much faster action than any of us had expected.

After lunching at a country store, most of the afternoon was spent cruising about the shoreline, checking on the success of other fishers. Near a small village where a large circular area of water was enclosed all the way round, except for a narrow channel through which it had backed in, there were many boat and bank fishers. Every few minutes in one direction or another we could see the bend of a rod and the subsequent jumping of a bass. In the two days the lake had been open, this village area of water had already become a favored fishing ground. While standing on a small bridge from where these observations were made, I looked down at an incoming branch that moved slowly along through the front yard of a house and settled into an almost dead spot of deeper water fifty feet above the bridge. A largemouth was making his way above the bridge. In the spot mentioned I left a bucktail, but not until I had added that bass to the bag.

Late in the afternoon we crossed the long French Broad River Bridge and spent another hour at a boat-dock just beyond. During that hour I don't think any of our party had ever seen so many bass come to dock in so short a time (aside from Florida waters). With ease, everyone seemed to be taking a limit. The catches were a combination of large- and small-mouth bass, pan fish, and sauger. Among the many fishermen coming in to dock, there were nine who ignored everything but bass. They displayed seventy-two of the fattest bass, length considered, that one could imagine. I had never before seen bass so plump. The heads gave proof that their bodies were outgrowing their heads. I have seen many bass the same length that wouldn't exceed half the weight of those first-year Douglas bass. Of course, the abundance of food was the only answer to that. This was one trip when we didn't have to take our fishing seriously—not the best of sportsmanship, perhaps. The next day it was the same thing; we found excellent fishing by just cruising about the lake and stopping at odd points here and there.

Naturally, this quality of fishing would seem too good to be true and could hardly be expected to last over an extended period of the season. Those first opening days of a new lake, when fish are nearly sure to be abundant, give an exaggerated idea of what the future fishing will be like.

During the summer of '44 and the spring and summer of both '45 and '46 I recommended this lake to several parties of anglers; several local fishermen also went over and fished it. Checking up on the subsequent reports, some seventy-five per cent of anglers visiting Douglas had fair to excellent success. Similar reports of continued good fishing, except in the dead of summer, came from fishers native to the Douglas region, and in spite of heavy fishing by thousands of anglers during the last three years, it is estimated that not more than ten per cent of the available fish crop is taken. Under present methods of harvesting, that seems to be the maximum take that can be expected.

In addition to the largemouth and smallmouth bass, crappie and other pan fish, sauger, or sand pike as they are sometimes called, are found in this lake. While not a large fish, the sauger is a tasty and desirable addition to the other varieties. Fishing can be fair the year round, but the months of March, April, May, and June are best. In very hot weather trolling and bait fishing are favored, but heavy stringers are more frequent in the spring months. Because of warm weather during mid and late summer and the probability of fall draw-downs for flood control, fishing is not recommended during July, August, and autumn. To give an idea of how many fishermen this TVA lake can accommodate, it covers an area of 30,600 acres, is forty-three miles from dam to headwaters, and has a shoreline totaling 556 miles; that, in a straight line, would reach from North Carolina to New York City.

There are other worthy lakes in this general region, such as Glenville Lake, south of the Smokies, which is trout and bass water, and

Lake Cheoah, southwest of the Smokies, a bass and pan-fish lake. East and southeast of Asheville, in the foothills of the southern Appalachians, there are several old lakes most worthy of mention here. Forty-five miles due east is Lake James, a body of water that has given consistently to bass fishermen for more than thirty years. Lying in a region where the mountains taper off to the hills and where the climate is milder than in the higher country, it offers very good large- and small-mouth fishing in the early spring. From boyhood I have fished this lake, depending on it some years for the early weeks of spring fishing. It has given me many fine fish. Lake James is a sizable reservoir, with its headwaters beginning on the Catawba River, just below where the stream comes down out of the mountains, and extending for a length of twenty miles (with the dam about midway) to where the Linville River comes in at the far end.

In the lower mountains southeast of Asheville is Lake Lure, the most beautiful of all the lower mountain lakes. Despite the fact that it is the hardest-fished lake in this state in proportion to size, it continues, season after season, to be good fishing water. Aside from the two basses, crappie, and bream, in the early spring a fair number of rainbow trout are caught. It is another body of water in which spring fishing is best. For years the greater portion of large bass coming from Lure have been taken during late February (when the weather is favorable), March, and April. Excellent examples of the large fish taken from this water in early spring are a ten-and-one-half-pounder and one weighing eleven pounds and seven ounces, during April 1947. Indeed, such bass are about as large as they come anywhere north of Florida. The larger one will perhaps take a prize or two in this particular region. My own best fish, however, six-, seven-, and eight-pounders, were taken in September and October. At the lower end of the lake the peaks give way sharply to the rolling country where cotton blossoms aren't far away, while at the upper end the towering mountains enclose the heart of a famous tourist region. Whether or not one takes fish, it is a lake that pleases.

Eight miles due south of Lake Lure is Turner Shoals, also known as Lake Adger. Lying in the "thermal belt" strip of country, conspicuous for its minimum of spring frosts, this is a wildish lake that I have fished for more than twenty years—more often, owing to the warmer locality, in March and April. Fishing there is either very good or so tough that it is difficult to take a single fish—like Lake Santeetlah, treated in the preceding chapter. On its better days I've always liked this largemouth and pan-fish water. Here, before passing from the lakes, and Turner Shoals in particular, I shall recount a youthful adventure that has remained fresh as one of my most thrilling experiences. What happened that day on my first trip to Turner Shoals was farthest from my expectations. No man ever had taken a fish by such complicated happenings of chance. No man ever would—that was the subsequent conclusion.

On that morning, more than a score of years past, my car was brought to a halt near the dilapidated barn at the upper end of the lake, which served jointly as a docking-place and sleeping-quarters for fishermen. Not having a companion on the journey, I was at once interested in a lone youth who greeted me. Someone would be needed to paddle along that beautiful shoreline. The boy must be bargained with or the trip might be in vain. A deal was made—one dollar for his services for the afternoon, on condition that he be allowed to troll his cripple-back as we moved along.

A short stretch of shoreline and two narrow strips of backwater were covered without result. Emerging from this last recess of cove water, we proceeded slowly down the north shore. Directly ahead were perhaps five hundred yards of straight shoreline well provided with cover. I had worked this water but a short distance when my lure became snagged in a sunken pine-top. The boy steered in the direction of the bank to release it. During the disengagement process there was a warning click of his casting reel and a swirl off forty feet astern. As he tightened up on the line, a bass came out of water in an attempt to throw the plug; not a large fish, perhaps one and one half pounds or so.

The youth shoved the paddle to my end of the boat, indicating that I was to take over while the play was in progress. Contrary to the urge of the average country boy to "horse" a fish in, he handled his equipment prudently. He seemed in no hurry to get the fish into the boat and was still giving line when the bass might have been brought to net. Finally he started to reel in, and as he did so, we were suddenly confronted with a complicity of events that had us groggy.

A dark streak appeared from the sky. My eye caught the object while it was still some distance from the water. For a brief second it had the likeness of an expended cannon ball directed toward the fish. It struck the water with a splash, and within seconds we saw wings open up as the predator attempted to rise from the water with the fish. The hawk became frightened at our nearness, but failed to get into the air with his prey, although several strong attempts were made. There followed a series of fast flopping maneuvers as the bird attempted to get free from the prey. Suddenly, however, he started skywards, quite free from the fish, but the reel sang again, and the line was going out and *up!* Instead of being fastened to a fish, the boy was now fastened to a fishhawk.

The hawk had become entangled with the hooks on the plug and, while we were absorbed with the struggle, the fish had got free from both the hooks and would-be captor. The boy applied pressure to the rod and thumbed the reel. The hawk kept to the air for a short time, going this way and that, striving to get free. When drawn near the boat, he would develop reserve power and start skyward again. In the confusion and excitement, time was forgotten. My memory fails me, but this air circus may perhaps have gone on for fifteen minutes—maybe longer—and when the bird was finally retrieved to the boatside he still showed plenty of fight.

Neither of us wanted any part of his sharp claws and razor-like bill. Retreating to the stern of the boat, the youth maneuvered his rod in such a way as to draw the bird over the side amidships. Between us we placed a board and the paddle on him and pressed him to the bottom of the boat, where we could safely unfasten the plug, which was hooked firmly in his neck. The plug removed, the question arose how we should dispose of our prize. It was decided then and there to tie up the bird for the time being, until we were through fishing.

With the boy holding the hawk to the bottom of the boat, I threw the plug, still attached to the line, out in the lake and started stripping off line. Not having the necessary cord for tying, my companion had directed me to strip off line till the other end was reached, which would serve well enough. He did not wish to disturb the outer portion of his casting line. This completed, I proceeded to tie the feet of the hawk. With one foot well secured, I made ready to place the line around the other foot and draw them together. At that instant the boy shouted: "You damn—" something or other. It was no mere skirmish on the outpost of profanity. He had become careless, and the hawk had plucked his hand, cutting well through the skin. To shake the bird loose, he upset everything but the boat. In that instant, and before we could regain our composure, the bird had taken off and was flying down that straight piece of shoreline.

An instant later the plug was lifted from the water beside the boat; one end of the line was thus fastened to one foot of the bird while the other was still attached to the plug. While tying the foot of the hawk, I had neglected to break off the portion of line needed. As we watched the hawk cover a hundred yards of water, the lure was first in the water, then in the air. A thought flashed through my mind: What a miracle it would be if a bass were to strike the plug! But this could hardly happen, even though a bass might be in the right spot and in a receptive mood—the flight was too swift. The hawk swooped down abruptly some two hundred yards away as if deliberately planning to alight on the water. He actually did alight, and with apparent force. Rising out of the water as suddenly as he had hit, the hawk perched on the bough of a dead snag some fifteen feet out in the lake. Cautiously we moved the boat in that direction. Presently I hit upon the reason that caused the bird suddenly to swoop down to the water during flight. The lure had struck some obstruction as the hawk flew along and he had been suddenly jerked from flight to the water's surface.

Hugging the bank so as not to frighten the bird, we paddled to within some seventy-five yards of the snag. By close observation the reason that caused the bird first to strike the water, then settle on the snag, became clear. We saw a bobble in the water between us and the snag. It was the plug resting on the glassy surface. Moving a bit closer, we could see the line leading from the plug to an overhanging limb, which came well out over the water. The line was fouled around the limb in some manner. The boy exclaimed suddenly that he could see the line running from the limb to the hawk. The plug bobbed again.

"What caused that?" my companion queried.

We moved closer, since the hawk now seemed little concerned with our movements. The plug bobbed again and again. By this time we had eased close enough for better observation. Again the plug moved sharply. As it did, I saw the limb to which the line was entangled wave slightly and, coincident with the movement of the plug and limb, I saw the line quiver and tighten between the limb and the hawk. The mystery was fast clearing up; the hawk by his movements on the snag was jigging the plug. We sat still in the boat, just watching, wondering when and what the climax would be. The hawk was perched about twenty-five feet above the water, his movements distinct and clear. Each minute gave me a better conception of the physical circumstances. Periodically the hawk would lower his head to his foot and peck at the line, trying to pick it loose from his foot, and each time he did, the line, thus tightened, caused the plug to jig. It was a beautiful job of jigging. He continued to peck and pull, several times in succession, to undo the line.

Forgetting the hawk for a moment, I gave my attention to the plug. With each jig a wave of water would widen from it in a large circle, only to fade on the glassy surface. At that moment our thoughts coincided. We had better frighten the hawk from his perch before he cut the line. There still seemed a remote possibility of again capturing him and retrieving the plug. We paddled toward the snag with our attention centered on the reaction of the hawk as we closed in.

Something that sounded like a minature explosion in the vicinity of the plug came to my ears. Instantly there was *another* splash as a large fish broke the surface. I could see the limb to which the line was fastened waving as if the line had been jerked violently. At practically the same instant the hawk left the snag and started across the lake. Whether or not he was jerked off or voluntarily took to flight I never knew. The line tightened between the hawk and the water. He was down, then up again, struggling either on the surface or a few feet above it to get into flight.

There was another break in the water, perhaps a hundred feet from shore. Yes, it was a fact—a bass on one end, the hawk on the other. There was little to do but let the fish and fowl have it their own way for a few minutes without interference. The bass broke water several times, and once or twice both were in the air simultaneously. Slowly but definitely they were exhausting each other. For some moments we kept our distance, just watching the performance. Neither of us seemed to have words suitable to the occasion.

Presently it was evident that the fish would eventually drown the hawk, which had already had quite a day before this last skirmish.

Removing the lure from my own leader, I tied on a treble hook. Several casts were required before I finally made contact with the boy's casting line. On the last break of the fish I cast crosswise between him and the hawk. Letting the treble hook sink in some depth, I retrieved and felt pressure. The hawk was drawn to the boatside and finished off with the paddle. The bass was practically exhausted, and I had less difficulty than I had anticipated in bringing him to net without the aid of the rod tip. He was a beautiful seven-and-one-half-pounder.

To whom did the bass belong? The hawk had teased him into striking by jigging the plug over his domain. He had been hooked with the boy's plug and played to a finish by the hawk. But still it had been my rod, line, and hook that retrieved the whole business. Two clean one-dollar bills influenced the boy to give me title to the fish.

I fished earnestly for several years before taking another bass as large as that one, but those which followed in subsequent years have been taken by more conventional methods.

CHAPTER XV

Tackle

A discussion of tackle in this book would seem little needed, especially since almost every tackle counter is laden with booklets treating the value of balanced tackle and the proper tackle for various waters and so on. No general résumé will therefore be attempted here, but only practical suggestions of what is most needed for the particular region. Many still go to the streams and lakes scantily and improperly equipped for the specific fishing to be had.

First, what fly-rods which may properly be classed in three sizes, large, medium, and small, are most suited for the streams of this general region? Two rods will answer the purpose for all streams. For casting to the larger waters, an 8½- or 9-foot rod will serve adequately. For these larger streams strong rods with a medium-stiff or stiff action are generally preferred. On the smaller streams rods of 7 to 8 feet are the proper tool; they fit the possible casting-distances and are more efficient in the brushy and overhung surroundings of these narrower waters.

About flies. For good reason the gray hackle comes first to mind. This well-known fly is a particular favorite with the natives. It has perhaps been fished more—wet or dry—than any other fly, and has brought more trout to basket than many others combined. The yellow body is generally favored, especially in the spring months, but other bodies are also effective. Next in popular favor with the natives comes the brown hackle and then the coachman, royal preferred (again, fished either wet or dry), and then next a sort of sedge-colored hackle. In the wet-fly category there is little more worth saying. The various patterns and styles of flies that will take trout in this region are too numerous to mention, but the standard patterns that are good in other regions are also good here.

As to dry flies, it would be hard to choose any single outstanding one. By all means, your fly-box should contain bivisibles, both brown and black, the browns in both light and dark shades, but you must also be sure to have royal coachmen, quill Gordons, Cahills light and dark, ginger quills, olive duns, and black gnats. Many others could be mentioned, but if you have these you'll catch your share of fish. If I had to choose only one fly, it would be a brown and white bivisible. If I had to choose *three,* it would be a brown and white bivisible, a ginger quill, and a quill Gordon. For brook trout a royal coachman is excellent.

During the middle and late seasons the spider fly may be put to excellent use. The fly referred to here is the flat-hackled, broad-spreading spider usually tied on not less than a No. 14 or 16 hook, as made by that master angler, Edward R. Hewitt. I have yet to see a native angler using this spider fly, for the simple reason that natives are not yet familiar with its use, which requires quite a departure from the conventional float of the common dry fly. On three of the Smoky streams I have seen Northern anglers demonstrate how killing this spider can be. In convincing performances on the larger pools of Hazel and Deep creeks (the larger pools being distinctly preferable for the necessarily long line, long fine leaders, and skimming action required in using this floater) I have seen the spider men leave the stream with a basket of fourteen- to seventeen-inchers, when other fishers came in with a few smaller trout. The shades most effective are the badger, solid grays, light and medium browns.

For wet fishing I think of the woolly worm first, with or without spinner, in any stream containing rainbow or brook trout. I'm not acquainted with any underwater fraud more killing. In recent years this woolly worm has become the popular stand-by of many wet fishers. Tied on an elongated hook, the sizes presently preferred—which may seem large—are eights and tens. They are made in many patterns. The long woolen body is dressed thinly with hackle and usually closely trimmed to a shoulder near the eye of the hook, where it is left full. From experience with these worms for the last eight years, the following colors seem to be most taking: the yellow body trimmed with gray hackle; the light-brown body trimmed as above; salmon-colored body with gray trimming; salmon body with light or medium brown trim. Other combinations, however, sometimes take trout about as well as those mentioned. The straight-eyed hook is greatly to be preferred, as it works better with a spinner.

Spinner combinations are common in most trout waters, and they are consistent takers, the spinner with attached woolly bug being responsible for more and larger fish than the spinner used alone. In almost any of the shapes and in sizes from 0 to 3, the spinner fly or spinner lure is a killing combination on all streams, my own preference being for the willow-leaf pattern as being easier to retrieve.

So far, nymph fishing in this area has been little explored. Nymphs are used very sparingly by the natives who, from lack of experience and application, are not too handy with this imitation of the stream-bed chrysalis. As with the spider fly, about the only ones known to be successful with nymphs are the visiting anglers, but even they do not use them often.

And now a word about fly sizes. The sizes predominantly favored in the regular dry-fly field are 10's, 12's, and 14's, the latter two sizes being usually preferred when normal conditions prevail.

Of course on some of the higher streams in late season when the water is low and gin-clear, such as Big Creek, upper Cataloochee, upper Forney's Creek, and a host of others, something smaller may be needed. Sizes 16 or even 18 may raise trout where the larger numbers fail. Tied to a 3X leader or smaller, they may often be put to good use. In the regular wet-fly category, sizes 8, 10, 12, and 14 cover the necessary range, but sizes 10 and 12 are the most used.

Regarding lake fishing, which is pursued with both casting and fly rods, there are several practical things worth mentioning. Since casting rods are not confined to the shorter distances, almost anything goes. But in fly, spinner-fly, and bug fishing, where the shallow margin of the shoreline and the shallow bays offer the most likely prospect, the longer, stiffer fly-rods, capable of good distance, are desirable. The length best suited to carrying a longer line is 9 or 9½ feet. However, an 8½-foot stiff fly-rod may be made to serve fairly well. Perhaps it should be mentioned that a line of sufficient weight to develop the power of the rod and straighten out the leader and lure to their maximum is an essential component of such a rod. Short or soft fly-rods have no place in this lake fishing unless one is devoted to pan fish.

About lures there is little to be said. The better-known makes, sizes, and styles of bass lures are also effective for pike fishing, and there are so many that choice is a matter of individual preference. Of course, lures suitable for the various depths of water, such as floaters, shallow, medium, and deep runners, should be in every bass fisherman's tackle-box, so that he will be equipped to present them at whatever depth bass are resting, but I greatly prefer to take my fish near the surface and only resort to deeper lures when all surface or near-surface lures fail utterly.

CHAPTER XVI

Rules and Regulations

In late years there have been some changes from time to time in the regulations governing the fishing waters of this general region, particularly the lake waters. As more has been learned about fish life and fish propagation, these changes and adjustments here and there are often found necessary to create a more equitable balance between waters that are over- and under-harvested. More recently, however, with competent fish culturists on the job, regulations are becoming more stable.

For the trout streams at large, the open season begins April 15 and continues through August 31. Trout streams in the refuge areas are open to fishing at stated periods between the above dates. All the TVA lakes treated here are open the year round; so are Nantahala, Santeetlah, and Lake Lure. Others at large are open from June 10 through the following April 15. As to lures for lake fishing, anything goes, and bait of any and all kinds is permitted. Aside from the bag limit and the minimum length, there are no other restrictions.

Going into the Smokies, the angler should know how the large body of streams are managed. The most necessary thing, of course, before stepping into any stream within the park boundary is a North Carolina or Tennessee license, or both.

At the park boundary line to most of the prominent streams, there is a sign, heavily columned by native hardwood, specifying the species of fish that may be taken, the bag limit, the minimum length for each fish named, the type of lures permitted, and the season during which they may be taken. *The use of bait isn't permitted within the park; neither are treble or gang hooks.* The approved lures, which are sufficiently broad, are the dry fly, the wet fly, and the spinner fly, with a dropper attached to either, and any artificial lure containing no more than one hook.

While the preceding regulations are now in force and have been for many years, it seems likely that there may be an experimental change in the near future. Just recently park officials submitted to the National Park Service a recommendation that, on a trial basis, bait fishing be permitted. Most officials seem to concur in the opinion that allowing bait would help to improve the fishing generally by ridding the streams of cannibal trout, which are difficult to take with fly-rod artificials and which feed, to a certain extent, on small trout. It is also felt that the approval of bait fishing would be of advantage to a large percentage of anglers who make no profession of being expert with the fly-rod. While there is some opposition to this anticipated change—coming mostly from fly fishermen—under the present stocking program and the limit placed on the fish, it is the claim of biologists that such a change would be no real threat to good fishing. At this writing, it is uncertain what will be done about this recommendation, but whether or not it is a wise move is a question that can be answered only if and when it is put into effect.

Streams in which the fishing has markedly deteriorated are sometimes closed for a year or two. Certain headwater prongs of the main streams are also closed for restocking, but information of this kind and current changes in regulations may be obtained from the rangers and wardens.

When camping overnight, a campfire is permitted, but from dead wood only or wood especially provided for the purpose. The ax or hatchet must not be struck into a green sapling—that is one of the regulations most stringently enforced. As a whole the streams are well governed.

The wardens are capable men, educated in their special field of work and well trained in their jobs. They can often suggest to strange anglers a more profitable stretch of water than the one being fished, or they can advise as to the most effective flies and lures for a particular stream or season. On the other hand, they can be tough if the occasion requires. A recent example of this is still fresh in mind.

Among a party of four on one of the favored park streams, one was a man who for a long time had been after me to go fishing with him. He was known to be a capable wormer—and a foxy wormer if circumstances demanded. I didn't like the idea and so wasn't present, but here is what happened.

On the way to the stream he concealed his flat tin of night crawlers; the others could fish their way, but he was going *down* after the big ones with his bait. He knew all the ins and outs of worming one certain stream, and that stream was Cataloochee Creek. His companions cautioned him, but he made no pretense of heeding them. He had night crawlers, he had, and he was going to use 'em. Besides *he* knew the wardens—stood in with them and could get a "fix" if it came to that.

At the stream he took a different course from the others. For his specialty the large pools of the lower creek were best. Everything went along fine for a while—three fine rainbow trout had come to his basket by midafternoon. Then suddenly his luck changed. While he was standing on the bank near the head of a pool, the back swing of his rod suddenly stopped. Turning his head, he was looking into the face of a warden, who was already stripping line and leader through his hands to become better acquainted with what was on the far end. Further close inspection revealed the tin can of night crawlers and a portion of one hanging from the mouth of a trout in his basket. Aside from the embarrassment of a J. P. fine and a suspension, he was a spotted man thereafter. Wardens seem to remember these characters, and once a fisherman has been convicted of a violation, they are likely to step out from a clump of laurel any time.

I saw a party of four men who were reported to have undersize fish searched by a single warden, and it was a thorough job. The length happened to be all right, but they had all exceeded their bag limits. These men had the physical proportions of tough customers, but the warden was entirely capable of taking care of them.

Strangely enough, I have yet to learn of a violation by a visiting out-of-state angler. Most such anglers are both willing and anxious to do what is expected of them. I am sorry that as much cannot be said for an occasional resident, who sometimes yields to temptations in the home park. On the whole, the wardens are an excellent body of men, practical, reasonable, and competent, and the fisherman who cannot get along well with them and *profit* by so doing had better examine the mote in his own eye.

PART THREE

Hunting in the Great Smokies

Author's Note

In the late eighteenth century buffalo and white-tailed deer roamed the valleys and coves of the Smokies. White settlers were few in those days, and the Cherokees put to good use their bows and arrows. With time the buffalo became extinct and the remaining big game consisted mostly of the black bear and the deer.

Today the deer population is substantial, but is confined largely to the various national forests. Bear are still abundant, and, as will be later discussed, they inhabit a large strip of the country that takes in a region of more than two hundred miles in length and half as broad. From recent reports of hunters and wild-life census-takers, there is even now some evidence of a gradual increase in their population.

In the early 1900's the Russian boar was successfully introduced into the wilds of western Carolina. This planting of Russian boar has been the most successful of all attempts to establish this vicious hog on American soil. During the years they have spread out considerably, and today their habitat includes a large area that overlaps into eastern Tennessee.

In addition to the big game mentioned, the native ruffed grouse is of much significance to the wing shooter. This important member of the rasorial family of birds is found in abundance throughout the whole of this mountain country and also rightly deserves a place in the chapters to follow.

As to the Smokies, hunting is not allowed in the park proper. At first this may not appear to the hunter's interest, but there are sound reasons for it. The park provides a huge protective shelter and breeding ground for game, especially bear. Owing to the park's heavy population of bear, many of them wander into the surrounding rugged areas and thus become available to the hunter. Bear will quite likely continue in abundance as long as this great breeding area is preserved, and this conservation policy seems likely to continue. Aside from the bear ranges near the park area, there are several sections of this general region that are famous in their own right as bear habitats.

For over a hundred years there has existed in this region a famous breed of game dogs, unique in the canine field. Until recently the breeders of this unusual dog have kept the strain confined to the Smoky area, where they were first introduced. Aside from the few out-of-state hunters who have seen these dogs in action, the breed is still strange to the American bear hunter. For both bear and boar hunters the history of this dog and his rare qualities warrant here a special chapter.

When October comes in this mountain region and the first heavy frosts begin to color the forests, there's much for the hunter to look forward to. My own days with gun and dog haven't been so numerous as with rod and reel, but they have been richly rewarded. Everyday acquaintance from boyhood with the region, its game, its hunters, native and transient, has left many clear and pleasant memories, and in what follows the aim will be to bring some of these to life.

CHAPTER XVII

Bear

Distinguished Hunters—Famous Bears

"Four bears and two Russian boars were killed last week by a group of western North Carolina men during a hunt in the Santeetlah area of Graham County. The hunters reported unusually thrilling experiences with the boars, which are among the most vicious game encountered by American sportsmen. Those killed had to be shot four or five times with large-caliber guns. Interesting encounters with game took place every day during the hunt. The group pitched camp between Lake Santeetlah and Tapoca Lake. Because the camp was near a highway, a large number of tourists stopped and viewed the animals killed."

The above is a typical news item of a combination hunt such as appears in almost any local Sunday paper during the fall hunting season.

For an idea of what bear hunting is like in western North Carolina, a sketch of several distinguished hunters, past and present, their feats in pursuing bear, how the bear country has delivered to the hunter for generations, and how the bear population has remained substantial through the years will perhaps best tell the story.

There comes to mind first the long-famed Wilson family, among whom great bear hunters have been a family tradition, from generation to generation. There *may be* in all America bear hunters who have achieved as great fame as the Wilsons, but certainly none who are more renowned. A century ago Big Tom Wilson, the biggest man in Yancey County, settled on the Cane River side of Mount Mitchell. In the very beginning, bear hunting took precedence over farming, and only enough land was cleared to supply the family needs. There, in a day when bear meat was a valuable supplement to the family table, Big Tom, slowly but surely, was establishing himself as the greatest hunter in the East. In the span of his spectacular career he killed a total of one hundred and thirteen bear. When his trusted rifle was retired to the rack for the last time, he had established a record that his friends claimed would never be attained by any other hunter.

Next in the family line to establish a truly great reputation was Big Tom's son, Adolph Wilson. Much could be said about this astute hunter, but perhaps the most fitting tribute that can be paid to Adolph is to recall his faithful reverence for his father's record. He was one among true sportsmen in the rough. Confident that no other hunter but himself could beat that great record, he prematurely hung up his rifle when he had killed his one hundred and twelfth bear, refusing even to go into a tie with his father.

Today Ewart Wilson, probably the most outstanding bear hunter in the Southeast, is living up to the family tradition. If his annual take of bears continues he will most likely retire when his one hundred and eleventh kill is reached. Possessing an uncanny knowledge of the bear and his seasonal habitat, Ewart continues to lead men and dogs into the vast Wilson Boundary. The annual take of bear in this mountain wilderness evidences the present-day claim that the brutes are as numerous as ever.

The unique records made by the Wilsons are not a yardstick by which bear hunters in general should be measured—their corn comes in a different half-bushel. It is quite a different story when you pass from theirs to the records of average hunters. Any man who has killed ten, fifteen, or twenty bears, and there are many such in this region, has established a very enviable record. Among the outstanding hunters was Mark Cathey, the famed trout fisherman who took trout and bear season in turn. When his days with gun and dogs came to an end, the bear notches in his gun rack totaled fifty-three, a magnificent record for any man.

A hunt in which Branch Rickey was a participant some years ago is a sample of how itinerant hunters have fared. When his party's three-day trip to the lower Hazel Creek area was concluded, out of the fifteen to twenty bear jumped, eight had been slain. Of course this is not representative of all hunts—not by any count. Sometimes there are no kills. Sometimes a single bear is killed, sometimes it may be three, four, or five; but, incidentally, a party of hunters made it seven from that identical Hazel Creek area in the fall of 1946. Anyway, on a long-range basis, heavy kills appear to average better there than in other parts of the country, if I have the records straight. When a noted bear hunter comes to this region, if he gets on well with the natives, sometimes the preparations are mighty, and when the occasion calls for it, the natives can usually show a visitor some moving bear meat.

Wherever bear are found, certain animals are singled out because of individual, frequently notorious characteristics. The three most prevalent characteristics by which these individual specimens become marked animals are: their huge size, their nocturnal excursions among the yearlings and porkers to satisfy a developed taste for meat, and their disposition to range over a wide area.

This region has had its full share of famous bears. Old Kettlefoot, named by hunters who claimed that a kitchen kettle wouldn't cover his footprints, possessed all of the wide-ranging, cattle-killing traits of an old animal. Old Kettlefoot's deeds in many widely separated pastures got his name into the papers often, but finally once too often. One New Year's Day when he left an undevoured sheep carcass in a Sugar Mountain pasture, the chase was on. That day was his last, and it ended for him at the mouth of his den.

Perhaps the most noted animal of the bruin kingdom is Honest John. For almost two decades he made the headlines. Though this bear has stopped much lead, he always managed to get his giant frame to safety, and it is reported that he is spending his declining days in the security of Smoky Park. This bear, reputed to weigh in the neighborhood of six hundred pounds, conspicuous for his huge tracks and the absence of a foretoe that was once left in a steel trap, never killed just for the sake of killing, but only to satisfy his appetite. Instead of making a fresh kill he returned to the scene of his slaughter and finished up a yearling killed a night or two before. By killing for food only, he came by his prefix "Honest." Season after season hunters from other states joined in the hunt for Honest John, but despite the evidence of his frequent engagement with calves and porkers, he was a wizard at evading men and dogs. Honest John wasn't just another big bear; his fame had indeed spread afar—so far as to attract the attention in 1935 of John Halzworth, chairman of the Alaskan Bear Committee of the New York Zoological Society, who came to western North Carolina to obtain information regarding his habitat.

The hunting and killing of large bear are always replete with thrills and not infrequently the loss of valuable dogs. One of the largest ever to inhabit this part of the country was killed in the Slick Rock Creek section of the Santeetlah region. He was an old animal, seen and hunted for a long time, whose hide had been the

A group of Swain County hunters and their bear dogs (a mixture of Plott hounds and Walkers) pose before a remote cabin prior to an outing, ca. 1920s. Note the bear and 'coon skins hanging behind them. Identifiable members of the party include, in the front row, Jonah Seay (fourth from left), Mark Cathey (sixth from left), and Sam Hunnicutt, author of Twenty Years Hunting and Fishing in the Great Smokies *(third from right). (Image courtesy of Jim Casada)*

Swain County bear hunters pose before a cabin (possibly at the Bryson place on Deep Creek) prior to a hunt, ca. 1920s. Two identifiable members of the party are Robert Snelson (standing, third from right) and Mark Cathey (standing, fifth from right). (Image courtesy of Jim Casada)

potential prize of every local bear hunter. Like most big animals that turn to the hog or cattle pasture to vary their diet, Big Black gained himself quite a reputation, but a reputation far beyond his carnivorous leaning. Of the many bear-killing tales, the finish of this particular animal is one of the most interesting. When Old Black's pay-off day came, his last act was in keeping with his dog-killing reputation.

One fall morning, with nine hunters and fifteen dogs participating, a hunt got under way. In less than half an hour a bear was jumped, but no one suspected it was Old Black. A native hunter, coursing the direction the animal was taking, started to cross Slick Rock Creek, from where he planned to climb a knob and intercept the animal, which was apparently headed in that direction. About the time he had reached midstream, it became evident that the bear had changed his course. With the water running well over his boot tops he stood there, undecided for a minute, but soon he heard the dog music "coming round the mountain" in his direction. Stepping up on a rock there in midstream, he found a good position for observation and just waited. As the minutes passed, the race came closer and grew louder. Presently, high above him, came a sound like a huge boulder rolling down the side of the mountain, cracking and breaking a path as it came, with the wail of a dozen dogs mixed in the wake of things. Standing there on the rock, the hunter saw the huge animal come into an opening, then turn and head straight down the opening toward the stream.

He had never seen a bear so completely covered with dogs. Two or three were at his head, several were snapping at his flanks, and two dogs were doing a good job of hanging onto his hams. Once, in the melee, a dog made an awkward jump, landing him for a few brief seconds on the bear's back. For a few paces he was actually riding the animal. Just short of the creek, the bear paused long enough to smack off a half-Plott hound high in the air and put him out of action. Abutting the stream, the bear burst through a clump of creekside undergrowth, which knocked most of the dogs loose. The instant he broke through to the stream bank, a high-powered bullet crashed through his heart. It is characteristic of large bear to kill every dog they can get at. Old Black, while in the act of falling, grabbed a hound in the back with a death grasp and crushed him as a dog would a rabbit, cutting him almost in two pieces. Later that morning it was discovered that two other hounds had been mortally wounded and left dying in the animal's path.

From midmorning until nine that night it took nine men to get the animal to camp, only two miles away. For hours it was lug a few paces, then rest, then lug again. The account of the killing of this famous bear went to press, but lacking in detail. The story was related to me, first-hand, by the aging hunter who made the kill and saw the bear in his last vicious act. The weight of this bear was reported to be six hundred pounds, and there's a country preacher's word to substantiate the claim, if that means anything. Without question, he was indeed a giant specimen of his race.

CHAPTER XVIII

The Black Bear

Habits and Characteristics

In the south Atlantic states hunters claim the existence of several subspecies of the black bear. In the various localities they are referred to by such local names as mountain bear, swamp bear, hog bear, and so on, but there is little justification for all the miscellany of names by which they have been described. There is only one black bear, and except for slight variations in color, prevailing more noticeably west of the Mississippi River, they are practically the same throughout North America. *Euarctos americanus,* the deep glossy-coated bruin of the Smokies, is the color purist of the North American black bear.

In spring and summer they frequently range close to populated communities, for days or weeks at a time, usually around the outposts of the mountain farms where tasty food is available. When they go on the prowl, which is usually when food gets scarce in the higher mountain ranges, they seem, surprisingly enough, to be about as much at home on the fringes of civilization as they are back in their own dense forests. Interesting reports of their foraging activities during the summer are common among mountain farmers. Many are the tales of a she-bear and her cubs having spent the summer nights in some farmer's backwoods cabbage patch, or corn patch when the corn is green; or how they have bedded down in the blackberry thickets in the daytime, from where they ventured on nocturnal prowls to include a loin of mutton in their diet. While averse to close contact with man, their many telltale signs are evidence of their deeds.

In the Smokies the fisher, hunter, or hiker may see trees clawed, bitten, and chewed by bear, sometimes so badly chewed that the tree subsequently dies. The observant hunter can form a good idea of the size of a bear from such trees, since a bear will chew and claw as high as he can reach. Various reasons have been given for such tree signs, but as reasonable as any, perhaps, is the influence of mating season, at which time the tree becomes the victim of male wrath.

In the Smoky Park, where they are protected and where their numbers are great, they have become accustomed to people. There they are indeed a bold animal. For years it has become a habit with tourists to share their lunch with the bears. This has become so common that some of the bears expect it. There is no doubt that they have learned to associate the parked cars along the road with food; so much so that they have come to be quite tame along certain stretches when lunchtime arrives. More than once they have been known to climb through the windows of vacated autos in which food has been left, with no hesitancy about helping themselves. They never molest a human being unless teased or influenced by food, in which case one cannot well depend on just what they will do. Tourists frequently get too bold with them, forgetting that they are, after all, wild animals, and, at times, park visitors have received ugly wounds about the arms and shoulders. Such incidents are responsible for the prominently displayed road signs of recent years prohibiting the feeding or molesting of these roadside bears.

The young are born during the months of January or February.

It is said that they are sometimes born as late as the first weeks of March, but little evidence seems to substantiate that. Most of them are born in January. One, two, or three may constitute a litter, usually two or three. At birth they weigh less than a pound. Their mother is always in hibernation when the young are born, and excepting the necessary forays to satisfy the family appetites, she remains in or close by the den until the young are of a size and agility to follow her in search of food. In the spring, by which time the cubs, still young, have attained a weight of between five and ten pounds, she begins to range them near the den. As they become older and better able to get about, she gradually takes them farther afield. In the fall following their birth they hibernate with their mother, but the following spring, having passed their first birthday and reached a weight of from seventy to one hundred and ten pounds, they either go off alone into the wilds or are driven off by the mother. June and July are the mating times, and normally they bear young every other year, but when the mother begins to age, there is a longer lapse between her mating seasons.

In many ways and for many reasons the black bear is one of the most interesting of our wild animals. Some years ago I had the opportunity of peeping on the activities of a Smoky she-bear and her three cubs. On a warm sunny afternoon in the month of June, on a small tributary of Hazel Creek, I was casting for trout. Something like two hundred yards up the smaller prong I heard a noise in the woods out to my right that sounded like the cracking or breaking of a dead log. Stepping from the stream to the edge of the thickly grown bank, I soon found what was going on. A thinly wooded V-shaped glade extended from its widest extremity down near the big creek to a point some distance above where I was standing. Near the lower end were the remains of a cabin, formerly used by fishermen. Glancing in that direction, I saw a cub bear emerge from the side of the cabin, and about that time another log-cracking noise came from out in front. A black bear and another cub were working energetically about the debris of a partially rotted log. They were about two hundred feet away.

Cautiously I moved a few steps forward, and presently the first cub from the old shack showed up at the log. A moment later, about fifty feet beyond the log, a third cub appeared, about six feet above the base of what I took to be a wild walnut tree. This cub was evidently practicing climbing trees. Back at the log, the mother bear appeared to be busy raking up food of some sort— grubs or other insects. At intervals the two cubs were taking brief helpings as she saw fit for them to be served. They were really tearing up things around that log, and finally the third cub joined the party.

I had never had a better opportunity to observe close at hand the pranks of an adult and her young. A soft breeze coming from their direction was of course the reason why they didn't discover me. In such remote sections they are especially keen-scented, particularly as regards man, and when he is about, they become highly alarmed.

After a few minutes the mother abandoned that portion of the log where she had been so busy and began clawing at the other end. Presently she turned the log on the ground, but, not satisfied with that, she took her paws and, to my amazement, uprighted one end of a broken chunk of the log larger in circumference than she, and longer too. For a second it appeared she was going to shoulder it and carry it away! Her motive, however, was soon revealed; she began ripping and tearing it apart for the grubs it contained.

In the meantime two of the cubs were back at the walnut playing like two puppies in a barnyard. One cub followed the other up the tree for a distance of about ten feet to a limb convenient for their pranks. In one of their playful clinches they both came tumbling to the ground. There was a bawl from one of them, causing the mother to straighten up and look, but soon she was busy with her log again. It all came to an abrupt end when one of the cubs started in my direction, perhaps for water. Fifty feet from me he stopped, turned, and made double time back to mamma.

Sensing something wrong, she immediately assumed a standing position, scenting for an enemy. That was to be all, for with something of a warning grunt to the cubs, and before I could realize it, they had disappeared in the heavy forest up the creek.

Perhaps the most common characteristic of the bear is his willingness to accept almost anything in the way of food. Bear are largely vegetarian, but they also know their way around a sheep pasture when the grape pickings are a little out of reach. The variety of food they will eat consists of berries, fruits, grass, roots, acorns, vegetables, honey, grubs, insects, fish, frogs, turtles, eggs, poultry, pigs, sheep, and beef on the hoof—quite a menu for their year-round sustenance. All this food is available here, and frequently the mountain pasture or apple orchard supplements the berry patches and grapevine thickets of the higher ranges.

The adult bear is definitely a solitary animal. Excepting a mother and her cubs, they never range together. The natural life span of the black bear is something like that of a horse. They live several times the age of maturity, but some live much longer than others. The natives have certain ways of identifying old animals that have been marked by traps or other means. It seems well established that many survive fifteen to twenty years, perhaps longer. The black bear is primarily a deep-forest animal when gun and dog season arrives. Chased by a pack of hounds they may carry this chase several hours, sometimes a full day, but sometimes they come to bay quickly, particularly a young one. Their short claws are adapted to climbing, and they usually take to a tree.

As will be discussed in the succeeding chapter, the Smokies and the neighboring ranges of the surrounding area are acclaimed the most famous bear habitats and hunting grounds in the East.

CHAPTER XIX

Bear

Ranges—Season—Guides—Division

In the Smoky region there are several mountain ranges acclaimed as the *best* bear-hunting grounds. The bear population is widely scattered, but, as might be expected, the greater numbers of the annual kill come from within the refuge areas. These refuges, in which hunting is permitted periodically and where the hunting is best, are the Big and Little Santeetlah drainage areas of the Nantahala National Forest, Sherwood Forest, the Mount Mitchell Refuge area, occasionally some portions of Pisgah Forest, and the Tellico Plains Refuge area of the Cherokee National Forest—the last, the only one of the above on the Tennessee side of the Smokies. In addition there is the private holding of the famous Wilson Boundary, mentioned elsewhere, on which for generations the bear population has been consistently abundant, and where many hundreds of bear have been killed by both native and visiting hunters.

The season in this region normally begins October 15 and continues through December 31. This applies to any open territory *not within* the refuge boundaries. The major bear hunts are the co-operative hunts arranged and supervised jointly by the U. S. Forest Service and the State Department of Conservation and Development, with hunters selected from a drawing. These hunts are usually conducted during the months of November and December. Dogs are always used in these hunts.

The guide is the key man of the hunt. After the party is organized, guides are selected for their ability to handle dogs, their knowledge of the region, their acquaintance with the most probable stands, if there is to be a stand, instead of following the dogs. On arriving in bear territory, the guides (after placing the hunters on the best stands) begin what is known as the "jump" part of the hunt. With the aid of assistants, one or two going in one direction, the others in another, they begin the search for "bear sign." With the strike dogs on leash, they start up the heavily timbered coves and ridges. Frequently the dogs are kept on leash until there is evidence that a bear has been in the cove, or until the dogs pick up a fresh scent. Occasionally the wise old-strike dogs are turned loose and given a free rein to search out the country, strike the bear, and yell his whereabouts to the mountain-tops. When that happens, the other trail dogs are released and the real chase begins.

Several outstanding hunters of the countryside have served notably in the capacity of guides. They are Nath Birchfield of Robbinsville, North Carolina, Sam Birchfield of Tapoca, North Carolina, and Newt Hooper of Robbinsville, who, as mentioned in a later chapter, have also established reputations among boar hunters. Ed Sanouke, also mentioned elsewhere, has led many bear-hunting parties. Then there is the famous Wilson family, of Burnsville, North Carolina, who have guided hundreds of hunters into their private seventeen thousand acres of bear wilderness. Ewart Wilson, often referred to as the King of Eastern Bear Hunters, is the present leader of the Wilson clan. There are others eminently capable in this capacity, but those named are excellent contact men when contemplating a bear hunt.

When the hunt is concluded and the animals are butchered— a procedure that takes place sometimes at the camp, sometimes at a convenient spot close to where the kills were made—it is quite interesting to note how the hunters arrive at an equitable division of the meat. An ancient rule is adhered to strictly: hunters making the kills do not come in for any greater share than others participating in the hunt. When the number of hunters is ten or twelve or upwards, and the quantity of meat is limited, the accepted mode of division is this: if, for example, there are fifteen hunters in the party, the meat is cut and arranged in fifteen neat piles. The quality of the cuts will run choice, middling, and poor, and quality gives way to quantity, the less desirable cuts making the larger piles. The hunters usually stand by until all are in agreement that the lots are equitable; then one of the hunters may be blindfolded or required to stand behind a tree. At that point the spokesman points to a pile of meat and asks: "Who gets this pile of meat?"—The hunter behind the tree calls out: "Bill Trigger" or "Tom Balsam," and so on as the meat is pointed out, until the division is completed.

Sometimes the hunters are few and the kills are numerous. For example, ten or twelve hunters may have a fine day or two of it and kill four, five, or six bears. In that event the above procedure is by-passed; there may be half a bear or slightly less for each participant. The guide is recognized as the legitimate claimant of the bear hide. Since a bearskin is just another hide to him, he usually auctions it to the highest bidder or sells it to some hunter who needs a rug for his den.

There are many recipes for preparing bear meat. On the mountaineer's table it is served in a variety of ways; it may come from the kitchen in the form of a juicy pot roast, or it may be hashed brown giblets filling a biscuit pan. In some of the remote mountain communities the boneless meat is even preserved by canning so that it may be available the year round.

CHAPTER XX

The Russian Boar

American History—Characteristics

For years the introduction of the Russian boar into the Smoky area was a controversial subject among Tennesseans and North Carolinians. Some claimed that these wild boars were imported from the Black Forest of Germany. Others contended that two North Carolina brothers brought several of both sexes from Russia shortly after the first World War. All this controversy has added much glamour to the presence of these rugged animals. While the country from which they were first imported is still highly conjectural, the facts concerning the time and place of their introduction has been quite well established.

In the early part of this century an Englishman named George Moore leased a large boundary of forest land adjacent to and including Hooper's Bald, a wild, remote and hard-to-get-to region of the Smokies. Upon Hooper's Bald, the highest peak of his holdings, he enclosed a large timbered tract with a great fence. He had visions of creating a huge, unique game preserve. On the slope near by he erected a big lodge, kennels for his dogs, and various accommodations for the friends that he expected to hunt with him.

One afternoon in the year 1910, mountaineers from the surrounding country gathered on Hooper's Bald. They came to see what was in the heavily bolted crates that had been transported to the high peak. When the crates were opened, there was a frenzied rush for the trees—it was every man for himself. The natives had never seen the like of wild beasts that scrambled for the woods in every direction. The Englishman's collection included boar, bear, buffalo, elk, and other smaller game. Of all the animals released, the boar attracted the greatest attention. It is reported that right there by the crates one of the boars, before making for the woods, ripped open the stomach of a bear that got in his way.

With the passing of years there was much fence-cutting by the natives who wanted to share in the big game. Gradually the buffalo and elk disappeared, and, as the natives had prophesied, the Englishman's visions of a big-time game preserve were doomed to failure. But in the end there was at least some return for his efforts. The Russian boar, as it has since been called, was a hardy animal, and the interstate wilderness of western North Carolina and eastern Tennessee (admirably suited to its propagation) became the habitat of this wild hog. It was in the early twenties that I first began to hear about the boars, which by then were solidly established in this wildest range of Eastern America.

The boar's physical make-up is unlike that of the domestic hog; its body is narrow, sloping from powerful shoulders to small hams. Underneath long dark-brown or black bristles, which are split at the ends, there is a closer woollike coat. This physical characteristic is evidenced that the boar was once the genuine native of a cold region. Possessing great strength, endurance, and size it is the biggest and most powerful of the wild-hog family. In the physical sense it is superior to the wild boars of Malaya and India. Two distinctive features of its make-up are the red glint in its eyes when fighting (which fades soon after it is killed) and its razor-like tusks, its chief weapon of attack, which in adults range anywhere from three to six and one half inches long.

This boar is the most vicious of all animals that roam the American forests. *These* red-eyed piggies don't go to market every day in the year. The black bear is no match for this powerful brute. Not a few old she-bears, foolish enough to pick a pig for their cubs' dinner, have been found with their entrails ripped and strewn from nose to tail. Backed to a ledge by a dozen or more dogs, he displays a come-on-in-and-I'll-take-the-pack-of-you disposition. He can slash a path to freedom where he pleases. Ill-tempered and shortsighted, he fights at close range with a charging and ripping tactic. In contact with dogs or other animals the boar operates with a lightning-like upward thrust of the head; in the flash of a second the sharp tusks are swung into action in rapier-like fashion and the damage is done. Of all American big game, boars take the greatest toll of dogs. In this region surviving hounds, curs, and the various breeds and mixed breeds used in the chase carry more scars than hunting dogs in any other part of the country.

A few years ago a report reached me that seemed not only most unusual but an exceedingly rare example of a hunter's ingenuity where the life of his dog was concerned. It is the tale of a mountaineer who was the owner of a better than average boar hound. As the story goes, his fine dog, not satisfied with the usual amount of hunting with his master, would go out alone among the ridges and sometimes spend the day swapping a little dog meat for wild pork. One afternoon about the time this mountaineer and his son were getting ready to slaughter a sheep for the family larder, he heard his hound whining in a fence jam on one side of his barn. When he came to think of it, he had missed the dog since the day before. He stepped quickly toward the fence jam, and as he walked up, a brood sow scurried from the spot where the dog was lying helpless. He observed that the dog's belly was split wide open, and part of his insides were hanging from the ugly rip. The dog, completely exhausted, was unable to rise to his feet but he recognized his master and as a token of this recognition he tried feebly to wag his tail. The mountaineer wondered how the dog had ever made his way in from the high-up ridges. Kneeling beside the badly beaten hound, he recognized what had happened—it was the telltale gash of a boar. Old Snaggle Tusk had done his work; he had slit the hound so viciously that he had almost emptied him inside out. But what was more puzzling, a single piece of the dog's intestine was riddled to bits. The mountaineer wondered if his barnyard sow hadn't taken advantage of the helpless dog and added to the injuries already done by the boar. Gathering the hound up in his arms, he carried him to the back porch of his house. The dog appeared to have little life left, but the mountaineer was determined by any and all means to save him if it could be done. There on the porch he administered treatment in a fashion never before heard of in these parts.

Looking out to the sheep lot, he called to his son, who had been waiting to help with the slaughter of a sheep. "Now, listen, jus' do what I tell you," he yelled to the boy. "I can't leave this dog. Knock that sheep in the head—stick 'er to bleed 'er, like you seen me do. Be in a hurry 'bout it—cut 'er guts out and bring 'em here t'me."

"Don't you want 'er skunt first, Pa?" the boy called back.

"T'hell with th' sheep's hide, she can be skunt later. Do's I say and git them guts here t'me," he shouted back to the boy.

By the time the mountaineer had washed out the dog's inner cavity with warm water and had got a needle and thread ready, his son had complied with the unusual demands. With the boy holding the pained dog's head against a folded sack, this native of the boar country, who had used the needle many times before, got ready to repair his hound. With the family scissors he carefully trimmed away about twelve inches of punctured intestine. Next he cut from the sheep's vitals a piece of intestine similar in length and size to the portion removed from the dog. After cleansing with warm water, he carefully sewed sheep into dog. Then putting everything back inside the understanding hound, he stitched up his belly, thus completing the unusual job of surgery. The hound was in one piece again with a little sheep for good measure.

That night the dog slept on a sack by the fireside with a pan of milk close by. The next day he was able to move about just a little, and with time he fully recovered. It is reported that this same hound chased boar for several years thereafter, but he was too wise a dog ever to get caught in close quarters again. Needle and thread are now an important part of the boar hunter's equipment, and the natives seldom go on a hunt without being thus prepared.

There was a time when the death toll of the boar dog in action was so serious that it became of great concern to the hunters. Many are the reports that, for example, from a litter of ten pups, bred to fight and put on the trail of a boar at the age of a year or more, after two or three hunts only one, two, or maybe three dogs were left. Not infrequently, however, one or two young dogs from the same litter, learning by the hard way of less than mortal wounds, grew wise and stuck it out with the boar for several years.

Some years ago a clan of hunters on the Tennessee side of the Smokies declared war on the boar. Their constant loss of many fine coon dogs that knew no better than temporarily to abandon the coon chase to get mixed up in a hog fight (when the stronger boar scent crossed the coon trail) prompted such action. But in the end their decision to rid the country of the short-tempered pigs availed little. Their campaign to "shoot like hell till the boars were cleaned out" or at least reduced in numbers was a total failure. Efforts to breed a great fighting dog that could master the boar amounted to little more than wasted time. Up to the present day there is one breed of dog, however, that has survived better than the rest and today is considered the best of the lot for this hunting. It will be fully discussed in a later chapter.

The breeding habits of the boar are not timed as seasonably as the bear's. From available reports, their mating season is spread over a longer period of months. The few occasions when a sow and pigs have been discovered were usually in the spring and summer months. In the winter, when the sows are heavy with pigs, they lose some of their speed and are frequently brought to bay much quicker than the males.

The litter may number anywhere from four to eight or nine; six or seven, however, are considered a large litter. On occasions where boars have been bred in captivity, the litter has rarely exceeded four or five. When she is suckling the young pigs, the sow maintains constant watch over her brood, usually denned up in the crevice of some ledge or cliff, or in some high thicket-like jungle of the mountain that is impenetrable. She is alert to all potential dangers, and when necessary for her to feed in order to suckle her pigs, she ranges close by where she can quickly sprint back to her den in case of an alarming squeal. It is reported she always bears the litter in a region where food will be readily available during the suckling period and until the young are of a size to take to the range.

There was a time when the U.S. boar population—divided between the Smokies and California—was estimated at less than a thousand, with the Smoky region given credit for the greater numbers. The most prolific of all American big-game animals, they multiply rapidly. Because of their habits and the remote regions they inhabit, an accurate census is difficult, but today they are spread over thousands of acres. Now permanently established, as one season follows another, there is evidence that their numbers are annually becoming greater.

There seems to be a difference of opinion about their life span. Some assert that the age to which they live and thrive ranges anywhere from six or seven to fifteen years. The fifteen-year maximum, however, may be exaggerated; on the other hand, it may be true with some individual boars, like the extreme longevity of other individual members of the animal kingdom. Anyway, the adherents to the longer life span base their claims on the fact that boars don't reach full maturity for several years, after which they still continue to grow and take on weight, similarly to a domestic hog when ranged in a pasture instead of pen-fattened. Other factors support the belief that they stand the years well. There are instances where a very large or a very vicious boar has been seen or been run by dogs for a long period of years. A few of them have been marked; for example, one may lose either of his tusks or have his tail chewed off by dogs. A few years back one huge specimen was given credit for killing more than a dozen dogs over a period of years. The native hunters have a unique way of spotting and recording the characteristics of individual animals, and what they tell you about them is not far amiss.

The size and ruggedness of the boar add much to the glamour of the hunt. One interesting feature about him is the large size he attains. Most hunters, when they first go into the boar country, presume the boar to be a much smaller animal than the black bear. We'll see about that. In this region it is claimed that the bear on an average will run no better than 200 pounds, which, to me, seems on the light side in estimating our black bear. The largest boar ever killed in the Smoky country was reported to weigh 600 pounds—quite a hunk of hog. While many small pigs in the 100- to 150-pound class are killed (young pigs that had not learned to lead the dogs into the dense ledges where man could not follow), 200- to 350-pound specimens are quite common. A fair example of size is very fresh in my mind.

One night only last week I was late in attending the meeting of the North Carolina Wildlife Federation. When I walked in I happened to take a seat by Ed Sanouke, an Indian guide, who knows the Smoky boar and bear habitats as well, perhaps, as any living man. I had been seated only a moment when Ed pulled from his pocket the curving tusk of a boar that had been smoothly sawn from the jawbone of a recent kill. He proceeded to tell me about a hunt in which he had just participated. It was one of those combination bear and boar hunts in the Little Santeetlah Creek section of the Joyce Kilmer Forests, where the timber is big, where both bear and boar range the same region; the kind of hunt where dogs trained to run whichever animal they strike first are used. On this hunt the bag was five bear and two boar, a good example of what the region gives to the big-game hunter. Two boars totaled 600 pounds, a 300-pound average, which was higher than the average weight of the five bears. Almost every year boar ranging upwards of 300 pounds are killed. It is these big fellows from 250 pounds up that keep the weight average high. Fisherman who go up the streams of the ridge country claim they have seen huge animals that would top 500 pounds.

I'm reminded that so far nothing has been said about the speed of the Russians. It may be hard to believe of a hog, but they have terrific speed. While there is no proof of the old saying that they can outrun a deer, they do run like a horse, and in the roughest sort of country their agility is incredible. When the chase is on, one may cross the ridge above you this minute and two minutes later be fighting the dogs on a ridge nearly a mile away. When a big one is first jumped in thickly grown country, he sounds like a little cyclone splitting through the rhododendron jungle. In terrain that would seem almost impossible to negotiate, they have an uncanny way of opening up a path. They frequently outdistance the hounds, leaving them to chase by scent instead of sight.

Rare indeed is the hunter who won't agree that a bullet through the brain or heart does not bring almost instant death to any species of animal. However, if you travel around enough, you can still get an argument on that, especially the shot through the heart. Most of the quaint tales of how much lead this or that species of animal can carry could well be charged up to poor shots, flank shots, crippling shots, clean misses, and so on. But the stories of the boar's capacity to keep traveling after absorbing more than any one animal's share of hot lead are not without some basis. Hunters will tell you of the boar's ability to keep moving for some distance after a direct shot through the heart. It is not uncommon for them to keep running for some minutes after high-powered slugs have punctured their intestines, until the loss of blood, contributing to the death wound, finally gets them. They have been known to keep fighting after a bullet has pierced the spine. There's something else that stamps this courageous animal with a Spartan characteristic: in the fight they never give a complaining squeal; neither will they squeal when pumped full of lead.

During the Russian boar's thirty-odd years of existence in the Smokies, they have occasionally interbred with a local strain of free-ranging razorbacks, which in their own right are pretty rugged customers. Evidence of this razorback blood is present in various degrees, ranging from the barely noticeable changes in the foreign strain to the more obvious physical characteristics of the native animal. This interbreeding has in no sense detracted from the sport of hunting them. The animal leaning to the native side, however, is not quite so speedy afoot.

Not long ago the experience of a man, alone in the forest, who by an unusual chance encountered a boar was related to me. While this experience was not one of battle between man and beast, as might just here be anticipated, it was of such a spine-chilling, hair-raising nature that it is of interest to any man who might tramp the ridges inhabited by these animals.

On a warm afternoon in the mid-fall squirrel season a native of the boar country began to climb the long ridge that led to the better squirrel territory. Near the top of the ridge he sat down in a flat grovelike spot populated with nut-bearing hickories. That afternoon the squirrels didn't come out to feed as expected. After a time, under the influence of a warm sun, he decided to nap awhile on a fluffy drift of leaves.

He didn't know how long he slept, but some time later he was brought to semiconsciousness by the cracking and popping of roots. After drowsily turning his head to one side, the dark form of a large animal standing motionless came into his hazy vision. His eyes opened wide. Not ten feet from where he was lying, the largest boar he had ever seen was standing still—still as a statue of stone, with not a bristle out of place, looking directly at him. His first impression of the boar was one he never forgot. The animal's head was down—down low—and two white tusks that protruded several inches from the lower jaw sparkled like ivory—there within a hog's jump of him. It was one of those rare occasions when a man is too frightened to feel his fear; it was more dangerous to be afraid than not afraid, for one wrong move precipitated by fear would bring on the charge. For minutes he lay there not moving a muscle or revealing a breath of life, and for minutes the boar stood there, just as solid and motionless as if he had been carved of stone. Between man and beast there was not even the batting of an eye.

In those moments which seemed so long, the mountaineer thought of his .22 bullets and how little impression they would make on that huge hog, even if he was quick enough to get the draw. He thought of his family, his farm, and other things. But he reasoned that the boar hadn't discovered him till he turned his head in the dry leaves, and that if he lay motionless the animal, so far not unduly disturbed, might refrain from charging. Watching the red glint in the boar's eyes and alert for any sudden change in his disposition, he planned, in the event of a charge, to spring up like lightning and race to a near-by sapling that he had in the course of his thinking selected for such an emergency. Time seemed long as the boar held his position as though just planted there, in a sense seeming to say: "Come on and do something about it." Eventually the boar turned his head a little, but it was his head only that seemed to move. From the corner of his eyes he kept looking at the man on the ground. After another moment or two he showed signs of becoming nervous, and the hunter knew that it wouldn't be long before he did one of two things.

Presently the boar sidled off a few feet, then turned and looked straight at him again. Shortly he began to move about, but every time he moved he always turned to take another long look. At a distance of some thirty feet he began slowly to circle the man, stopping every few feet to have another look. To the man (who had turned his head slightly so he could follow the beast with his eyes) it appeared that the boar was making plans for a snorting charge on the slightest provocation. At the same time he showed no disposition to come in and start things himself until he was given some excuse to do so.

Finally the boar began making his way up the ridge, but very slowly, as he was undecided about what should be done. About the time the native thought everything was safe, he rose to a sitting position. Up the ridge a hundred feet or so the boar stopped suddenly, turned and looked back. Slowly he retraced his steps to within fifty feet of the man, who by then was standing with rifle in hand, but ready to take a tree if necessity demanded. It was quite evident that the boar wasn't satisfied with the state of things. Again he turned away and at last disappeared up the ridge.

This particular boar might have been just curious or bewildered, or he might have preferred a good fight. Anyway, something certainly was going on in his thinking processes. It was a highly interesting example of the various characteristics boar display. On another day, like a fast express, he might have split the laurel wide open getting away, or, on the other hand, he might have charged viciously. Unlike the black bear, you can never tell for certain just what a Russian will do.

CHAPTER XXI

Hunting the Boar

When a party of hunters go into the interstate wilderness to hunt boar, they are going into something quite different from the simple everyday dog and rabbit chase. Only hunters who have tramped and climbed through the remote mountain jungle inhabited by this animal and who have lugged and poled a heavy boar—sometimes miles from where the kill was made—to the nearest mountain roadway know just what it is like. Coming to me recently was the story of a boar hunt on the Tennessee side of the Smokies and the kill of a 420-pounder. Some days later one of the participants in this hunt, Paul A. Moore, staff photographer for the Tennessee Department of Conservation, who made the kill, gave me a picture that helps to give some idea of the true size of the animal. The details attending and climaxing this particular hunt are typical of the rugged character of this hunting.

When Paul and his companions got together on the Tellico Mountain Plain that autumn morning, as at the beginning of all boar hunts, no one knew what might happen before the sun went down. Paul had long wanted to kill a big boar, and that morning, with four experienced dogs, one of them a hog-wise, hog-fighting Airedale, he and his party started the hunt on a strip of the most probable terrain. They didn't have to wait long for action; one of the dogs soon made a strike and the rest joined in. At the beginning the chase lacked the vicious action of a running battle

—the dogs were trailing by twig and track; the boar was out there somewhere, but just where or how far ahead was a question that the dogs must eventually answer. After trailing eagerly a mile or so across ridge, up and down slope, suddenly all hell broke loose. The far cry in the wilderness and the fierceness of that cry told the hunters that the boar had been jumped. It was then a different tune, easy to recognize when the dogs caught up with the hog.

For awhile a fast race was on; then it slackened and the voices of the fighting dogs, as if they were tied down to a certain spot, gave evidence of the fierce battle that was taking place. But soon again the voices of the dogs as they circled the far side of a ridge, then growing louder as they came across the top again, told that the boar was moving on. After another mile or so of dog-race-boar the fight was on again. As usual, this was a fight-awhile-run-awhile boar. For hours the chase and intermittent fighting continued over a large area of the wilderness, the dogs several times getting out of hearing. In the meantime the sound of battle indicated that there was more than a little swapping of dog hide for bristles and pork.

As the morning progressed, aside from the occasions when the animal stopped to have a few slashes at the four dogs, mile after mile of wild region continued to slide under the sure-footed boar. The voice of one dog faded from the chase. Not long afterward the deep cry of a second dog dropped out. The hunters knew what that meant; by stopping to mix it up now and then, the boar was slowly but surely taking his toll of dogs. The fighting chase continued, but a short time later a third dog was silenced, and the lone bark of one dog that had been constant all morning now told the story of what had happened to the three others. One by one they came limping in, badly cut, their blood-streaked bodies showing ugly gashes anywhere the cutting tusks had happened to strike. Finally, in the afternoon, the hunt ended in a darkish laurel thicket on a steep slope. The faithful Airedale, left to take care of things by himself, continued to bark when the boar stopped in the thicket to rest. When Paul Moore worked his way into the sloping thicket, the dog was as glad as any fighting dog could be at the sight of man and gun. He had seen boars go down at the crack of a rifle before and he seemed to understand that it was going to happen again. With a 30/30 rifle, at a distance of not more than fifteen feet from the hog, Paul pressed the trigger and ended the hunt.

The spot where the animal was killed was a good ten miles from the starting-point—a good distance even in a straight line, but added to the many circles and winding runs around ridges, up slopes and ledges, it had been, as a mountaineer put it, "one hell of a wild chase." When the other hunters came up, the hog was tumbled down the slope to the cold stream of the North River and there dressed. After that, a five-mile hike by short cuts brought the hunters back to where they had left the car. Next it was a thirty-mile roundabout drive for the boar on North River. All this is a hard day's going for both man and dogs, but it is an example of what boar hunting is like—if one likes boar hunting.

All boar hunts are alike in some respects, but they are all different in others. One never knows what turn events will take. On all hunts where a kill is made, it is always attended by some singular experience, thrilling or spectacular and sometimes dangerous; a different experience from the last, and one which, in the run of many seasons, will never happen the same way again. One such hunt that was quite different from all the rest, one that was guided by a hunter who has pursued the animals longer than any other man I know—from thirty years back, when the boars first began to take the country—may be recounted here.

Will Orr, who has lived in the boar country all his life and who acted as a guide for natives twenty-five years ago when the beast was unknown to the outside world, was in charge. One December morning during the early forties Will and ten other hunters met on Swan Meadow, near the head of Big Santeetlah. On this particular hunt the eleven dogs equaled precisely the number of men. Will had reason to believe that a large hog, along with smaller ones, was ranging in the Swan Meadow area. On previous hunts some of the animals had been killed in that section, but one large hog had been jumped that always got away, managing to rip up the bellies of a few dogs before doing so. One dog in particular that Will highly prized, a dog that was part Plott hound, had been carved badly by Old Snag, a name given the animal by Will. The gash had split his breastbone wide open, although he mended to live, much to Will's surprise; but he refused ever to nose a boar-scented twig again. Aside from that, this boar received credit for several other hounds that failed to return from the chase. Will hadn't yet seen the animal, but he had seen big tracks, and roots torn from the ground, and other signs that satisfied him Snag was a mighty big hog.

The hunt began that morning with two parties of men, who, with dogs on leash, started up each side of a laurel branch in the direction of Stratton Bald. An hour later, near the top of Stratton Bald, Will's jump dog, Jack, a crossbred Plott and redbone, suddenly winded toward a laurel thicket and strained at the leash. Before Will could unsnap him the dog began lunging toward the thicket. Once free of the leash, the dog went straight to where the hog had bedded up for the day. From the noise of the get-away, like a whippet tank crashing through a canebrake, Will was certain they had jumped Old Snag. Soon all the eleven dogs were in the race, but as usual Snag soon put a good strip of ridge between himself and the hounds.

For a mile the swift animal outran the dogs; then suddenly

the race came to an abrupt stop—they had caught up with Snag. While the hunters, led by Lee Orr, cousin of Will, made their way out the ridge, a fierce fight was taking place. When, after a time, the hog didn't move on, Will wondered if it *was* Snag, who had always been good for three, four, or five miles between fights. Lee Orr was first to come in sight of what was going on, and, to his surprise, Snag was down. As he came closer, he observed ten bloody dogs in action, on top of a large boar that for the time being, at least, had collapsed and was down, making no fight of it whatever. For a brief moment Lee's attention was drawn to a whining dog lying out to one side. That dog had good reason to whine. He had a bloody gash that started at the bottom of his belly and ended near the backbone.

Something was amiss—this wasn't the usual Snag. Never before had the Orrs known any number of dogs to hold a boar to the ground. Occasionally, when a boar has gorged the night before, and in the early morning before he has voided his kidneys, his speed and fighting qualities may be appreciably reduced. Whatever the reason, this time Snag had quit.

Lee Orr was poorly equipped for dispatching this hog, but with his finger on the trigger of his .22 he approached slowly from the rear to the downed animal, which couldn't be shot from any distance because ten chewing dogs almost obscured him from vision. From the look of the situation Lee gained confidence and walked into the midst of things. Between dogs that were having a heyday of it, he put his rifle barrel against the ribs of Snag and pumped three .22's into his vitals. As is characteristic of the animal, at the crack of the rifle the beast didn't flinch, but to be sure of things Lee thought he'd better step to the front of Old Snag and put a bullet in his brain to finish him off. Never before had he seen one of the wild hogs give up and accept defeat while dogs were chewing on him. Just then it occurred to him that he might have been wounded a day or so previously by some other hunter. That thought was short-lived. To his utter surprise, just as he was about ready to draw on the animal's skull, he saw the big hog's eyes open wide.

At the sight of man, and before Lee had time to think, the animal sprang to his feet and gave a tremendous shake that slung and scattered dogs in all directions. His rise from the ground and shaking off the dogs as if they were no more than dry leaves were a lightning-like action that took place in the batting of an eye. Lee didn't know what force it was that moved him, but instantly he was running for it, regardless of direction, so long as he was just going. He became conscious of Snag's vicious lunge at him, which knocked the rifle from his hands into the air. Three bullets were deep in him somewhere, yet Snag was after Lee with full power, and several dogs that were doing their best to hang on did little in the way of slowing him down. A glance over the shoulder revealed Snag close behind, and Lee knew he'd be a goner in a second or two unless a miracle happened.

In his fright he had no time to take cognizance of the ledge just below him; his only thought was to get to safety. Before he realized it, he was almost abreast of a big water-drained slickened rock that shelved off from a clifflike ledge to a dangerous bottom below. Like a flash Lee's quick thinking dictated that he make a turn, but he was going too fast to turn, and if he slowed up one instant the boar would be on him. Guided by some involuntary physical reaction to this extreme emergency, without knowing how he did it, he grabbed a bush and swung to the side of the steep-sloping rock out of the animal's path. The boar was making such speed he could neither stop nor turn. By that time another hunter had come up and was in a position to see Snag as he went over the rock, hitting here and there, trying to dig his feet in and regain his balance as he went down, but able to do little about it until he reached bottom, a hundred feet below.

Amazing as it was, with three bullets in his vitals, and after this half-fall, half-tumble over a steep hundred-foot ledge, Snag appeared as alive as ever, and when the dogs got down to him he was ready to fight. But soon the dogs had him down again, and a few minutes later a shot through the brain finished him off. He was too big to get out in the usual way by means of a pole, which was tried but found useless. Will Orr, who has lugged and helped lug many hogs out of the Santeetlah wilderness and who knows hogs and hog-weights as well as any man, estimated Old Snag as a good four-hundred-pounder. To get him out of there the hunters had to butcher him and cut him in chunks; then, with the chunks swung on their backs, it was a six-mile tramp to the nearest negotiable roadway.

When an inventory of the dogs was taken, there were no fatalities, but it was found that not a single one had escaped without a slash of some kind. One dog was too far gone to rise to his feet and had to be carried out, while two others were crippled and had to make it on three legs. Just why Snag failed to give a better account of himself by killing a dog or two and getting away this time was an unanswered question. But to the sweet satisfaction of eleven hardy hunters, it was a climactic end to Snag's dog-killing days, the inevitable end that comes to big hogs once they have been spotted.

CHAPTER XXII

Boar

Localities—Regulations—Guides

During the middle thirties boars became so numerous they were hunted for meat to supplement the native smokehouse larder as well as for sport. Any time was open season where the mountaineers were concerned. In spite of this illegal practice they continued to increase. In recent years, however, adequate protection has been provided. Aside from isolated occurrences, this illegal pursuit has been abolished in favor of carefully supervised hunts.

Today the approved method is as follows: There are two large refuge boundaries lying astride the border of North Carolina and Tennessee, comprising the Big Santeetlah area and the Little Santeetlah area of the Nantahala National Forest on the North Carolina side, and the Tellico Plains area of the Cherokee National Forest on the Tennessee side. These areas are jointly controlled by the U.S. Forest Service and the Department of Conservation and Development of North Carolina and Tennessee. Through these departments, hunts are arranged whereby qualified guides may take a party of twenty-five or less into the joint controlled refuges. A fee of fifty dollars is charged for such a hunt, which, on a per-man basis, is negligible. On these hunts a participant is allowed two boar, and if he is lucky enough to stop two in one day, he is through for the season, two being the season's limit per man. Bear are also allowed to be killed on these hunts, but the hunter who kills a bear is then restricted to one boar, or vice versa if a boar is bagged first. The season during which hunts may be arranged is between October 15 and January 1. Frequently, out-of-state hunters participate. The only requirement for them is the proper license and the approved caliber of high-powered rifle. Those not acquainted with the region usually have connections with native hunters, who act as their guides.

These co-operative hunts combine men and dogs, the party numbering anywhere from eight or ten to twenty-five, and the number of dogs, under present regulations, not to exceed eight. When the hunting party consists solely of hardy mountaineers, it is without question the roughest sport in America. They follow the pack of dogs into country that would be quite impossible for flat-landers. The usual procedure with visiting hunters is the stand hunt. By long experience the natives have learned the probable path, direction, or ridge a boar will take if he chooses to run for it instead of fighting, provided he is jumped where he is expected to be jumped. Accordingly, visiting hunters are usually placed on stands, and ordinarily the guides try to follow the chase so they will be close at hand if the animal chooses to fight it out, or is bayed in a ledge.

In addition to the man and dog hunt, a new kind of hunt was introduced in the fall of 1946, which, to begin with, met with the immediate approval of hunters. The purpose of this new arrangement is to stimulate public interest in hunting without the use of dogs. An example of how these hunts are conducted may be of interest here.

Under the supervision of the refuge management, two days are set aside for each hunt. The time is normally during October or November. To participate in one of these hunts it is necessary to make application to the North Carolina Division of Game, Law Building, Asheville. Each applicant must submit with his application a check or money order for fifteen dollars, which will be refunded if his application is not chosen in the public drawing. Applications, if not too great in number, are usually considered in the order received. Hunting is allowed during the daylight hours only and only rifles of .32 caliber or larger are permitted. Each person participating in the hunt is allowed to kill one boar. No other game of any kind may be killed on these individual hunts. Whether or not the dogless hunt will become a fixed custom is highly questionable. Such hunts lack the appeal of the trailing and fighting hunt with dogs. Several guides I've talked with recently aren't very enthusiastic about the new idea. Since the wild boar, unlike the domestic hog, prowls largely at night and beds up during daylight hours, they maintain that without the aid of dogs it will be much more difficult to dislodge the animals from the ivy and laurel thickets where they bed up.

Aside from the arranged hunts in the refuge areas, boar are sometimes hunted on privately owned land in the same general region. In the course of years the animals have widened their habitat, spreading out to the ridge country beyond the boundaries of the national forests. Mountaineers owning land adjacent to the boar country sometimes hunt in solitary fashion, like the squirrel hunter or the turkey hunter, for the occasional hog that roams during daylight hours. Occasionally they learn (by telltale signs) where the animals are ranging, and from an advantageous position just sit and wait for a shot. The outside areas are also hunted with dogs.

Hunters wishing to participate in one of the supervised boar hunts must make their plans well in advance. Prior to the fall hunting season, details may be obtained through the North Carolina Division of Game, as mentioned elsewhere in this chapter. For out-of-state hunters, competent guides are in a position to make the necessary arrangements. Among the skilled guides most familiar with the region there are Newt Hooper, of Robbinsville, North Carolina, Nath Birchfield, of Robbinsville, and Sam Birchfield, of Tapoca, North Carolina. Last, but not least, is Will Orr of Santeetlah, North Carolina. Will has successfully guided hunters from many parts of the country. He keeps a pack of good dogs that are especially trained for hog hunting, and when October 15 comes he is always ready for business. Despite his thirty years in pursuit of the boar, he can outtramp most younger men. Through his wide acquaintance with all regions inhabited by the boar, both the refuge areas and private holdings (he knows much about the latter), he has established quite a reputation for finding and jumping the animals. Highly regarded as a guide, he perhaps knows the hog country as well as any living man. More often than not kills are made when he is in charge. On a recent visit to his place I examined the scars on several of his ten hog-dogs and counted the skulls of seven boars lying around his woodpile, the remains of kills that were made during November 1946.

In America boar hunting is comparatively new, but in parts of Europe and Asia it is one of the oldest known sports. In ancient times the Greeks thought highly of the beast. His fighting courage was so regarded that several kinds of boar hounds were bred for this hunting.

CHAPTER XXIII

The Plott Hounds

Among American hunters the subject of trailing hounds is one of constant pros and cons. Of an evening in a bear hunter's camp it is not uncommon to hear the qualities of this or that breed or crossbreed of bear hounds argued and chewed to bits. The question of hound quality may center on such breeds as the black and tan, the bluetick, the spotted hound of Georgia, the redbone, or even the cur; or it may be a crossbreed of any of the above, with the Airedale or bulldog for strength, courage, and fight or the bloodhound for nose.

In a picturesque little farming community on the southeastern fringe of the Smokies where the Plott brothers live, which has been the native home of the Plott hounds since they were first brought from Germany, there is no argument about which is the superior of all bear and boar hounds. Over the years this outstanding hound has made the name Plott prominent among dog men of this region and, in recent years, the far-away states of Iowa, Montana, and other points west.

A good many years ago I first learned of these hounds, and the unique story of how they first came into being in the dog kingdom was quite contrary to the facts. The oft told story that their savage fighting qualities were born of wild blood is a myth that emanated from the now moldy fable of a wolf breeding in a mountain-shack chimney-corner with a cur bitch. The authentic history of the Plott hounds, which comes by way of my personal acquaintance with two of the Plott brothers, is this:

About the middle of the seventeenth century Johnathan and Enoch Plott, of Heidelberg, Germany, came to America and settled in the Smoky wilderness. They brought with them a pack of bluish brindle hounds that had back of them the blood of the cold-nosed *Schüssehund,* a strain of German hound. The several generations of Plotts that followed continued to breed these dogs in the original pure strain, but just to see what would come of it they also crossed their hounds with curs and other trailing dogs. More than half a century ago Mont Plott crossed his hounds with the dark leopard-spotted bear hound of Georgia; but in the end he wasn't satisfied with the Georgia cross and he gave the mixed breeds to his hunting friends about the country. Vaughn Plott, one of the present-day descendants, contends that the majority of the hounds scattered through North Carolina and Tennessee, which he classes as a hot-nosed dog, are products of the crossbreeding by his father, Mont. Several years before his death in 1924, at the age of seventy-five, Mont gave to his son, Vaughn, his entire pack of pure Plott hounds, which had never been interbred with any other dog. As a consequence Vaughn Plott is the present-day purist in strain breeding.

The first generation of Plotts were pioneers among the early bear hunters of the Smokies; in fact, they so loved the bear trail that breeding dogs for profit was of lesser importance. This is why the dogs were little known to the outside world prior to the last decade or so. Mont Plott, who, back in the eighties, blazed many trails into the Smokies, was perhaps the greatest bear hunter of his day; but his hounds were a factor in making him so. His chief weapon, quite unusual for a big-game hunter, was a cap and ball, musket-loading handgun, an antiquated affair with twelve-inch barrel. But his hounds were a kind that could stop a bear and tie him down so close in a fight (his sons claim) that the elder Plott could walk in when he pleased and dispatch the animal. Back in those days much of Mont's hunting was done in the Black Rock section of the Cherokee Indian Reservation. On these hunts he would leave home the day before, without his dogs, for Black Rock —ten miles away—where he would set up camp. At an appointed time the next morning his wife would unleash two hounds, which by cold scent and a keen sense of understanding knew just how to find their master, and soon the chase would be on.

Today the Plott brothers will put their hounds against any breed in the country. They are a dog of great speed and courage and can handle a trail on either dust-dry or frozen ground. When a Plott hound strikes a bear or boar trail, the valleys and ridges slide swiftly under his fast feet. A steady, long-winded all-day trailer, he can always be heard crying the way he has gone to the mountaintops. In a close fight with a bear this Plott hound has no equal in fierceness of attack; at least that is an undisputed claim in these parts. When a bear is once bayed, they frequently hold him to the spot, giving him such a tough time of it that his dripping tongue and foaming mouth bespeak his exhausted frame when the hunter arrives. In the thick of battle the great courage and fighting ability of the pure strain Plott is acknowledged by all. However, some hunters contend that the cross of a Plott with a black and tan, red-bone or bluesick, often results in a better strike and trailing dog. Various accounts of the Plotts indicate that the bitches are not inferior to the dogs. In a fight they are often the more aggressive.

The only account ever coming to me in which dogs conquered a wild boar was related to me by Vaughn Plott. In 1942 he was in the mountains with two bitches, which unexpectedly jumped a young boar. In a matter of minutes the dogs had split the boar's ears to ribbons, and his hindquarters were streaming blood. The dogs seemed to sense that the boar had not yet developed his tusks, and every time he made a jump to run for it, one bitch would swing to the south end while the other sampled ear meat. As the minutes passed they were fast getting the best of the animal, for one time turning the tables and carving boar, instead of being carved. About the time the exhausted boar was ready to give up and let them chew pork for a while, Vaughn arrived at the scene and, as a reverse of the usual order of things, rescued an out-of-season pig from his dogs.

In addition to bear and boar, the Plott hounds have proved their worth on the coon trail. It has recently been reported from out west that they have been tried on the cougar and have exhibited rare courage in hunting this member of the cat family.

The weight of a Plott hound may run anywhere from forty-five to sixty pounds; a few have reached sixty-five pounds and one was known to tip the scales at sixty-seven. It is a large-boned dog, possessing a broad chest and medium-length ears. On a visit to Vaughn Plott's farm in January 1947 I measured the height of three adult dogs and a puppy. The adults measured twenty-four, twenty-five, and twenty-seven inches respectively, from the ground to the crest of the shoulder. The puppy, which was four months and six days old, measured seventeen.

The color of the pure strain of these hounds is a dark molish or bluish, with more or less brindle mixed in. Some of them are of almost solid dark color, while others may have a prominent brindle chest and a greater or lesser belt of brindle across the back. While this is the predominant color, about ten per cent of the puppies have a buckskin color when born, which they keep through life.

The Balsam Plott Hound Kennels receive many letters asking about the history and hunting characteristics of these dogs. When puppies are available they sell them, and sometimes they part with an adult dog. The supply, however, is always far behind the demand.

CHAPTER XXIV

Deer

Coming as a youth to the mountains of North Carolina, I soon learned that the deer-hunting methods practiced there were quite different from those of the coastal flats. There the hound did most of the work, and the hunter could ride to his stand on a horse or mule and wait for the buck to pass within range. Often it was possible to ride through the scrub pine and gallberry thickets and jump a fat buck. Horses and mules were conditioned to the flash and roar of the shotgun, and no one walked where he could ride.

In the mountains, however, the rifle replaced the shotgun, and shank's mare supplied the transportation. The mountaineer, although conditioned to the rugged terrain, seems as much opposed to strenuous hunting as his coastal counterpart, and he has evolved many easy methods of obtaining his venison. The simplest of all (and it may leave one wondering if it isn't too simple) is the ease with which one of my esteemed fishing and hunting companions bags his deer at his country place in a setting close to the Pisgah National Forest. His back porch, screened in picture-window style, looks out on a green rye patch and a beautiful little mountain lake just beyond. On both sides of the lake the deer trek down from the higher forests to the green rye. When dusk falls, it is easy to turn from the card-table on the porch and through a hole cut in the screen above a two-by-four that serves as a rest, draw on an un-suspecting buck that has come down to feed.

Another unusual method of hunting deer is that employed by a friend with a sizable place bordered entirely by a strip of the better deer range of Pisgah Forest. On one side are several apple trees, which, when fall comes and the apples redden, the deer never fail to find. Beyond the apple trees is a four-acre field, entirely surrounded by the forest. The two things most common in this field during fall and winter are peas and deer tracks. The lower side of the field slopes down to the woods, and thick clumps of honeysuckle hang from a hedge of second-growth trees, furnishing additional winter forage. Overlooking the whole field and its bordering woods is a unique stand. This stand is reached by board steps nailed to an oak and leading to a plank seat concealed in the higher boughs. Fresh in mind is a December morning not long ago. A heavy snow covered the frozen ground, and a biting north wind was swaying the treetop. When the hunter was about to return to the cabin to thaw out, the only buck of the morning paused momentarily at the honeysuckle clumps. That pause was fatal.

Among the mountaineers are solitary hunters familiar with the various deer ranges. Among all Nimrods who stalk the deer, their lot, perhaps, gets the best of it. By preseason observation, or by a quiet word passed among their clan, they acquire the knowledge essential for the lone, still hunter in a brand of hunting pursued on the mountain ranges and farm lands surrounding the national forests, from which the deer range widely during certain parts of the season, especially when the high-up food crop nears depletion.

To get his one or two bucks, the native, usually before the opening days of the season, has spotted the daily path of a buck or a group of deer from which he intends to make his kill. Constantly on the lookout for "sign," he may spot a lone deer (not infrequently a solitary buck) or perhaps a small herd numbering five or six, crossing an open gap between two near-by local ranges of the greater range at about the same hour each day, usually in the late afternoon. Or for days he may keep track of a buck and doe that in the early evening have a habit of trekking the crest of his backwoods ridge on their way from one feeding ground to another. Once they are spotted, ranging the ridges or crossing the gaps, the solo hunter has little further difficulty. From a rhododendron blind or bushy cover at the base of a tree, or a thick tussock on a knoll, he gets set for the carefully planned shot when the deer walks into the selected opening.

One of the shrewdest of these lone hunters, as much a fixture to his native mountain region as the rocks are to the earth, is Ralph Stamey, who lives on the southern fringe of a deer range approximately three by eight miles in area, skirting the Pisgah National Forest. After hunting grouse and other small game with him for something like a decade, I've come to the conclusion that hunting is more of a vocation than an avocation with Ralph.

One December afternoon some years ago, while grouse hunting, we had come down in midafternoon from the higher ridges into a crab-apple flat that widened from the V-intersection of two branches. Ralph investigated an area that he had already indicated was at the time the nightly headquarters of a small herd of deer. His investigation was most careful and thorough.

"Five deer were in here last night, feeding on the crab-apples," he said, pointing toward the thickest growth of trees. Wondering how he had arrived at this figure, I asked: "Ralph, how do you figure there were just five?"

"The different sizes of tracks and the way they came in and went out. Out there," he said, pointing toward the V-intersection of the branches, "in the soft ground you can count the tracks where one followed another out of this flat. There's fresh tracks, made last night, and there's one big buck—his tracks are twice as big as the rest. I'll get him."

Ralph has an uncanny way of coursing deer to their beds. Pointing again to a broad, ragged area sloping down between two ridges, a half mile beyond the branch facing us, he said: "That's the way they went last night. They're bedded up in there today. Tomorrow morning I'm going to start my bitch through there. By the time a deer jumps, I'll be on this ridge stand, back of the flat here. When they jump in that snag slope, they'll take this ridge here out to the top, then head for the government boundary."

Ralph knew his deer—the next morning he got his buck.

For years he was owner of an unusual deer hound, one trained to Ralph's kind of hunting—an indiscriminate-looking bitch that understood just what was required when the leash was unsnapped. Often, when on this particular range with Ralph, he has pointed out the favored places where deer bed up during the day and told of the many times he's started his bitch into an area knowing the exact path the deer would take out of it. This, and his ability to time the dog's movements after coursing the first bark, is why he's the best lone-man-and-dog combination in these mountains.

In contrast to the legitimate ways most natives get a deer were the abject means formerly employed by the spotlighters and pot-hunters, whose depredations have now been greatly reduced by the rigid surveillance of game protectors. One of the most despicable of pot-hunter methods came to attention some years ago. One place favored by the nocturnal violators was a point near the shallows of the French Broad River, which separates the larger Pisgah National Forest from the well-preserved fourteen-thousand-acre Vanderbilt estate. On this estate the normal deer population may range anywhere from four to eight hundred. Near the shallows on the moonlight nights of the fall and winter many deer were killed while approaching or swimming the river from the preserve to the estate, or vice versa.

This account of deer hunting in the southern Appalachians results from twenty years' association with native hunters. The transient hunter, not familiar with this part of the country, should be reminded that a buck will not be quite so simple a matter for him as it is for the natives. With guides almost non-existent for hunting on the unposted areas fringing the national forest, his deer hunting had better be confined to the joint State and U. S. Forest Cooperative Hunt in the greater Pisgah preserve. After the closed 1946–7 season in western North Carolina, in addition to the opening of the region at large, these greater preserve hunts, which have in past years attracted so many interstate hunters, are to get under way again.

When the greater refuge hunts were first introduced, a surprisingly high percentage of the hunters made a kill. The following figures are of interest and may help to give a hunter an idea of his chances. During the first hunt in 1932, of 315 participating hunters, approximately 60 per cent made kills. On the next hunt, held in 1934, approximately 74 per cent of the 386 hunters got their deer. Of the 1,557 hunters taking part in the following hunt, which was in 1936, when bucks only were allowed, approximately 35 per cent were successful. On the next, in 1937, of 1,325 hunters, approximately 54 per cent came out with a deer. As a result of the wide publicity given to the above figures, the succeeding years produced many more applications than the Forest Service could provide for. Consequently both local and interstate participants were selected by an impartial drawing. In time, however, the high percentage of kills progressively declined to a figure that led to the belief that the deer population in the greater Pisgah Refuge area was rapidly reaching the vanishing-point. Quite alarming was the low percentage of kills during the early forties. Succeeding the first banner years, the gradual decline reached its low in 1943, when the take was only 91 deer for 1,200 participants. In 1944 and 1945 there was a promising rise in the percentage of kills, indicating a gradual upswing from the low of 1943. Partly responsible for the maximum decline was a change in regulations permitting only bucks to be killed. While hunters fail to understand the rapid decline over this period of years, the refuge officials concur in the following answer:

Prior to the first public hunt in 1932, the deer population in the Pisgah wilderness had thrived because they were in a protected region forbidden to the hunter. Thus, unmolested through the years, there was a huge build-up; their numbers increased far above the normal figure for that specific range. Accordingly, during the first few hunts the kills were abnormally heavy, leading hunters to believe that the number of animals coming from the government forest was going to continue to be large. The situation was similar to that of a trout stream which after years of preservation is opened to the public for the first time. Complaints from those unfamiliar with prevailing conditions caused much close-the-season talk. However, refuge officials contend that the deer life on the big range has merely been reduced from an overpopulated to a normal status, and this seems quite logical.

Throughout the southern Appalachians there are numerous national forests ideally suited to the white-tail deer. Besides the Pisgah Refuge areas, southwest and northeast of Asheville, with their 1,200,000 acres, there is in the extreme western tip of North Carolina the great Nantahala National Forest, with a gross area of 1,349,000 acres. Deer have been taken from the Nantahala, and it is now in the build-up process, so that in later years the hunting should be comparable to that of Pisgah.

In northern Georgia the Chattahoochee (comprising more than

a million acres) is another of the progressive national forests. Some years ago its stock of deer was sadly depleted, but at present there is a fair concentration, and this is now being built up so that excellent hunting should soon be available. Other national forests where there may eventually be good deer hunting are the Cherokee in eastern Tennessee and the mountain district of the Sumter National Forest in South Carolina. In view of the posted land, the wide-scale leasing of hunting rights, the purchase of hunting preserves by private clubs, all of which are absorbing much of the remaining hunting territory, the purpose of the public hunts in Pisgah and other national forests is to provide hunting for the average citizen who owns no land.

With intelligent management of our wide range of national refuge areas and the hunting therein, and with an overflowing deer population into the adjacent areas, present and future generations of hunters may confidently expect better and better sport.

CHAPTER XXV

Grouse

In western North Carolina the ruffed grouse is native to the forest just as the brook trout is native to the streams. Here, grouse hunting is one of the most inviting sports afield, especially for a hunter willing to go into rough country for his birds. The mention of rough country right here at the beginning of this discussion need not be discouraging, as a fair percentage of the early-season birds do come to bag from the lower mountain stubble fields and the lower coves and valleys. In the higher and rougher regions, however, they are found in greater numbers, and this in spite of natural enemies and the gunning season, is why they are considered our finest and most hardy game bird.

For one reason or another, the mode of hunting grouse in this area varies according to the individual hunter and is unlike the established practice in quail shooting. Of course, shooting behind dogs is the logical method, but many get their birds by hunting without the aid of dogs.

An example of what awaits the hunter who takes his grouse seriously may be given from my notes of a man who has hunted them steadily for nine years and whose annual kill has been just as constant and continuous as the turn of the seasons. I have personally seen most of his birds and learned the whys of his consistent success as compared with the annual three or four hit-or-miss hunts that are customarily my own lot. The rough character of some regions makes wing shooting extremely difficult, frequently reducing the opportunities to a single shot out of maybe five or six flushes. Only the ample supply of birds compensates for this, and naturally the smart hunter is going to hunt the areas that hold the greatest number of birds. Finding the most productive territory right at the beginning of the season seems to be the key to this hunter's success. Through the years he has become well acquainted with many of the better hunting grounds, and it is characteristic of them that an area supplying many birds one year may or may not be so productive the following year. When the season opens, he gets out for a day or two in the mountains, spotting localities where birds are most numerous, taking notes of food and other factors that may be helpful in locating their whereabouts.

The mountaineers can often tell him if there are many birds, where they have been drumming, what they are feeding on and just where he is most likely to find them. In this painstaking way he finally settles on the choice of a hunting ground, and unless there is heavy gunning by others, he sticks to the area selected until he gets his season's limit. I have known him to take this limit from one of such areas for three or four straight seasons before changing to another hunting ground. Once he knows the grouse are there, he hunts methodically and thoroughly. In the early season grouse are frequently found in coveys, but seldom is a covey found a second time on the spot where they were first flushed and shot into by the hunter. As he has proved, however, they remain in the same vicinity, though ranging more widely than quail. By covering the same general area on a wider scope as the season progresses, he constantly finds birds, singles, pairs, and so on, that have been broken up, one way or another, from perhaps several coveys.

Here is a fair example of how thoroughly he hunts out a locality when he knows grouse are there. In the season of 1946, after tiring a little of the territory he'd been hunting for the past three years, he decided to switch to a new hunting ground. Prior to opening day he was tipped off that birds were plentiful in a certain locality. He well knew that such tips are seldom reliable and that a confirmed grouse hunter (the source of his information in this instance) is careful not to reveal the secret of an extraordinary grouse range, so he decided to find out for himself. On the second day of the season he drove out to this territory, situated in the Cataloochee section a few miles southeast of the Smoky Park and extending for several miles on both sides of a small creek into a country devoid of human habitation, where the timber was semi-virgin and the going not too rough. Except for his dog, his was a solitary hunt. Leaving the car at an abandoned byroad at the lower end of the boundary, he started up the creek following what was left of an old grown-up lumberman's road to the right of the stream. In less than half a mile the setter gave signs of birds and came to a point on the edge of a thick scrub flat. As he walked in behind the dog, four grouse flushed. The three shots from his twelve-gauge automatic downed two birds, and right there—with little or no effort as grouse hunting goes—he had taken the daily bag. Before he picked up the two grouse, several others flushed. As he was making a further survey of the flat before returning to the car, the dog came to a second point, and a moment later two more birds took off. From a third point five grouse sailed out of sight across the ridge and two others up the creek. Before he left the area he estimated that at least twenty-five birds were flushed. Clearly he had found one of the better hunting grounds and wouldn't have to look further that season.

A few days later, this time with a companion, he went back for more birds. Experience told him that he need not expect to find coveys in the same scrub flat (they have a way of being somewhere else than where you last shot into them), but he did expect some birds. By working the area in circles, they found singles, twos, and threes, all not too far from the original find, and so numerous that only six trips were required for him and his companion each to get a season's bag. Of course, as the season progressed, wider and wider coverage of the territory became necessary, but I've never known him to finish a season without his annual limit.

(A find of fifteen to twenty-five birds in a given small area is known here as a grouse covey, but they are not a covey in the quail sense. While a single brood of eight or ten chicks do sometimes survive the predators and grow up and remain in covey formation until broken up by one means or another, the larger groups found in laurel thickets, berry patches, and flats are usually there because of the abundance of some highly prized food.)

An added reason for this grouse hunter's consistent success is the care he uses in his choice of dogs. For the more or less open country he prefers an old dog that has become slow afield, but that (essentially for grouse) retains a good nose and is steady among birds that flush easily ahead of a younger, faster dog (especially on dry days) that doesn't know his game. When hunting rhododendron thickets and heavy coves, he uses the same character of dog, but with a bell attached to his collar. By keeping alert to the dog's general whereabouts, the silence of the bell is indicative of grouse.

The bell-on-the-dog idea is an old device and has much merit in certain thick areas, as is well known among Northern woodcock hunters. It is used infrequently here, but usually it is a smart hunter that does so. In thick country the dog is often out of sight for minutes at a time, even at close range, and if he is dependable, an alert hunter can often maneuver from an almost impossible position into one for a probable shot, provided, of course, he marks the spot where the bell last sounded.

In this part of the country a dog is rarely trained solely on grouse.

More often a quail dog pinch-hits on the larger game, and most hunters prefer an older dog that has slowed down. Here, where the forest floor is dry much of the time and where a young fast-moving dog sounds more like a bull in the woods, the birds (unsteady even for the most careful dog) frequently flush far in advance of him, or of any dog that crowds in too close. Ordinarily, dogs of any age are willing grouse hunters; they seem to like the scent of the larger bird just as well, but few make really fine grousers unless trained for this purpose.

As for the matter of guns for grouse shooting, the twelve-gauge has widest preference. The reason for this is the heavier load, resulting in a thicker shot pattern and greater shock power, which the lighter guns with their lighter loads fall short of, when the bird is getting *on out of there.* My own hunting furnishes a good example. Many times with my pet twenty I have cut feathers or slowed up a bird only to see him go on, after a shot certain to have resulted in a clean kill had I been using my twelve instead. Frequently the effect of that one extra pellet from the heavier load makes a lot of difference in grouse shooting. In regard to shot size there is also some difference of opinion. For this mountain shooting some use fives or sixes, while others prefer sevens or eights. To judge from personal experience and the opinion of better hunters than I, the preference appears to be for a maximum load of $7\frac{1}{2}$ chilled shot.

In western North Carolina regulations for grouse shooting are the least regarded of all game laws. There are several reasons for this. First, wardens have no way of keeping an accurate check on individual hunters. The daily bag limit is two birds, the possession bag is four, and the season's bag ten—very simple figures—but there's no way to check on the hunter who gets his four birds on the second day of a two-day hunt or the hunter who goes out twenty times during a single season and kills perhaps thirty or more grouse. A good example of the little respect shown the regulations by local hunters came to my attention last fall. A college professor and one of his neighbors came in to tell me of a super grouse range he had found where he and his friend, the week before, had killed nine birds in one afternoon. As he talked, the open season was still two weeks away, but there was little reason to doubt his story.

Why this disregard for the law is more prevalent among grouse hunters (of course not all of them) is of some interest. A good percentage are dissatisfied with the short season and the maximum season's bag of ten birds. They reason that even in the more open regions only a small percentage of the birds are harvested, and that the predators get more than the hunters. They further contend that there are many immense remote regions where gunning is inefficient and where there are hundreds of coveys and thousands of birds that are never disturbed by the hunter. With (1) the birds having the advantage of these wild regions to breed in, and (2) the fact that less than fifty per cent of the territory can be negotiated by the hunter, and (3) the opinion of sound-thinking hunters who have studied the situation carefully and who contend that a longer period of shooting would scatter the birds to a wider area, thus reducing the interbreeding of family coveys, which some claim is undesirable, there does seem to be some basis for their contention.

Whatever the evidence in favor of the disobedient hunters, who know they are legally wrong but feel they are morally right, there is no disposition here to support their illegal practices. Changes in regulations should be made by the proper agencies, not the hunters. As things stand at present, however, it does seem quite plausible that the season could well be extended to January 15, with a daily bag limit of three birds. Only the crack shots would get the total allowed, and it would provide a longer period afield at a time when other hunting is closed and when fishing is negligible. This is a practical question of significance to grousers that I understand will be voiced to the Department of Conservation in the very near future. In suggesting that a slightly broader season would not be detrimental to the bird population of this general area, I'm quite aware of the grouse cycles that periodically occur throughout the grouse regions of North America. They are, perhaps, the most noted cyclic species of all our game birds. Nevertheless, the opinion of a substantial cross-section of our Appalachian grousers indicates that the decline during the leaner years is less pronounced, and never reaches the extreme low as it does in some northern regions. There's much evidence that our birds maintain a fair population balance. Not in my time have the various covers been without some birds. Should it ever come near to that—which I haven't witnessed during two decades of tramping about our grouse country—then, I will about face and strongly support a closed season for such a time as conditions demand. At this writing, however, and in view of the greater take by the various feathered and fur-bearing predators, the gun is not a serious factor in our grouse population.

As a final word, the ruffed grouse is the finest bird of our mountains, and every time I see one he does one thing or another that gives me a thrill. It may be the great speed at which he takes a ridge or the noise associated with his get-away that gives the impression of much bigger game than he really is; or it may be his way of putting a clump of laurel between him and me until he gets out of range, then sailing majestically down the branch. One morning in June 1946 I had the opportunity of seeing one put on a rare performance, similar to the mother quail's act when her young brood is suddenly faced with danger. But in the case of the mother grouse the "trimmings" were much fancier. At the conclusion of a morning's fishing on a high-up little brookie stream, I had just climbed up on the bank where the heavy timber gave way to a thinly grown knoll. My sudden appearance on the bank was a signal for an odd chatter, strange to me at first, until the origin and cause were revealed. Little streaks of only partly feathered young grouse were darting here and there and vanishing so swiftly before my eyes that I couldn't follow the path of a single one of them. The mother bird was feigning a near helpless cripple by dragging a wing and bouncing here and there to divert my attention. For some seconds she continued her warning chatter and dragged one foot through her widely spread wing feathers to convince me she really was crippled. Once satisfied that the little ones were safely hidden, she roared out over the knoll, alighted on a high spot of ground just long enough for a last look to see if everything was all right, and then took off for parts unknown. It was the smartest bird act I'd ever seen, and she had probably used it many times when foxes or wildcats threatened her precious brood.

In this region there is no sizable mountain range where grouse are not found. Of course, they are more abundant in some areas than in others, depending largely on food supply. As the population stands now, there are plenty for all who go after them. Here grouse hunting means rough going, but it is a great sport when you find yourself in a mountain sage flat or on a laurel branch with eight or ten birds flushing one after another and going in all directions.

CHAPTER XXVI

Squirrels to Order

The story now in my mind is of a squirrel hunter and the ordinary little gray squirrel common in all parts of this land. There is no pretense that squirrel hunting is of keen interest to itinerant hunters who follow the big-game trail, or that it is of more than table significance to natives of our mountain country, where the bushytail abounds. Nevertheless, this story is of a very individual brand of squirrel shooting which is so rare that it deserves a place here.

Unless I'm wrong, the world's best shots are natives of America. This covers a wide variety of gunmen all the way from the pistol expert to the skeet champion. There are many fine game shots, however, who have never seen a rifle range or a clay pigeon. I'm acquainted with a young mountaineer of this sort, known by the name of Coot, who lives on a sparsely settled mountain range south of the Smokies. In the professional sense Coot is an unknown, but in the strict sense of game shooting he is considered one of the best, even for this part of the country. When he presses the trigger, there is but one purpose in mind, and that is meat—he knows nothing else. We have all heard of the fellow who shoots quail on the wing with a .22; Coot may not be that good, but he does get rabbits on the run with his .22, and so far as I know, there is no hunter in his part of the country who gets more *game per ounce* of ammunition than he. That is his reputation, and it has long been common knowledge among his few mountain neighbors that a good portion of the meat served on his little kitchen table comes by way of his rifle. Before telling of Coot's rare brand of squirrel shooting it seems in order to describe the surroundings where he lives.

His cabin-like little house is situated in a four-acre flat by a small stream flowing down from the higher mountains. On turning the last bend of a sled road leading through a dark woodsy hollow to his place, one will very likely see a cow feeding on a stack of shucks, two hogs in a slatted pen, munching the remains of corncobs, and the cabin itself located on the laurel and holly banks of the stream. In good weather brook trout may be seen in a small pool sixty feet from the front door. A few game chickens scratching about the flat and two crossbreed hounds usually greet me on approaching the place. The bark of the dogs apprises Coot of your coming, and if it is a warm day the visitor will more than likely see him come out into the yard with two chairs in his hand.

After many trips to his cabin, during which acquaintance ripened slowly, I was taken inside. I was at once impressed with the thirteen sets of antlers, his trophies, choice sets taken from the mountain deer that had gone down at the pull of his trigger finger. The largest of these was from a fine buck that passed him on an occasion when he took a stand and let his bluetick drive through. This buck, he recalled, came near getting away—the cartridge snapped. After unbreeching fast and inserting a new load, he wheeled and brought him down. There you have the typical Coot.

But to get on with the squirrel story. One fall afternoon when he was occupied with his sausage grinder and some venison that was a little tough for ordinary cooking, he got a message from down the creek. There was a mountain neighbor, ailing and bed-fast, who felt that a mess of stewed squirrels might do him good if Coot could get them for him. To Coot, this was equivalent to an order for squirrels.

Fair squirrel shooting was available a short distance from Coot's back door, but he decided that a big hickory cove a mile and a half up the mountain gap, where squirrels were sometimes as plentiful as grasshoppers in a cabbage patch, would be the proper place to fill this particular order.

Arrived at the chosen spot next morning just a few minutes before the crack of day, he took a seat at the foot of a large "den" tree, a seat he had occupied many times before. A minute later an inventory of the pockets of his denim coat resulted in a bitter disappointment. Through a hole in his shell pocket six of his eight cartridges had been lost. It was a long way back to the cabin, yet he had an order to fill. While sitting there musing on this trying situation, squirrels began to appear in every direction, but Coot was in no hurry to fire his two remaining cartridges. He recalled many instances when he had felled two of the animals with a single load by merely maneuvering himself into a position where they both would be in line with his bead, or by catching two of them near together on a limb. With the passing moments, it seemed this was a field day with the squirrels. He could not recall any season when he had seen so many cutting in one hickory tree, where they all seemed to be gathering. In this tree and the immediate vicinity he counted upwards of thirty, and it still lacked some minutes before broad daylight. While all this was going on, Coot had resolved that at least three or four squirrels should come to his bag from those two cartridges.

Presently he had his first favorable opportunity; for an instant two of them stopped dead still when passing on a limb, their bodies almost as one. Taking advantage of this hairsplitting second, he fired. The result was one clean kill, but the second squirrel was only wounded and took to the den tree under which he was sitting, going into a hole some forty feet directly over his head. Coot was disappointed—only one squirrel, and just one load left.

After that first shot, things quieted down for a few minutes, but presently the squirrels were as numerous as ever. Sitting there waiting, he observed that one branch of the big hickory tree seemed to be the main squirrel runway connecting several near-by trees. His hunting instinct dictated that he keep an eye on this branch. Soon the second opportunity came. One squirrel was following another out the runway branch, and just as they came side by side at the fork of the bough in that brief instant when they paused before making the jump, a fast shot caught them squarely together, for a clean double.

Coot thought that was all for the day, but it wasn't. The two squirrels brought his total to three, but as he was putting them in his bag, a fourth came tumbling to the ground. Coot had just one way of figuring that out. There had been several squirrels higher up in the tree, and coincidentally with the double kill his bullet had tagged another squirrel in the course of its travel through the higher branches.

Quite satisfied with the turn of events, he stood his now empty gun by the trunk of the den tree and, hanging his bag of four squirrels on a snag, proceeded to the brook for a drink of fresh mountain water. Returning from the brook, he observed one of the squirrels on the ground near his game bag, yet he was certain all were stone dead when he had left them there. A look in the bag revealed all four squirrels still there. Coot was staggered by this discovery—he hardly believed it could be true. After what had already happened, it was indeed a rare day in his hunting career. The squirrel wounded by the first shot had crawled from the den tree where he had first sat down, and had fallen dead just below his game bag.

[203]

This was the only possible answer for that fifth squirrel. Anyway, the pay-off was five squirrels for two shots, an example of super-shooting and an unbelievable happening of chance, almost (but not quite!) beyond the reach of the imagination.

Here I think of the little mountain boomer, which belongs to the same family as the gray squirrel, but has some red among the gray fur, and attains about half the size of his cousin. Many hunters have never seen a boomer, one of the most interesting of small animals. There are many tales about the boomer, known for its amazing speed. It is claimed that one can chase another around a tree at such terrific speed that it looks like a solid ring of boomers, and that, as with the blades of a fan, the space between them only begins to take shape when the speed slackens. Mountaineers claim that they will frequently dodge the slower .22 bullet unless the hunter shoots when they are behind a leaf. But hardly credible are the tales of how, when lightning strikes a tree, they can beat it down and be halfway up another before it reaches the ground. The little boomer is unimportant as game, but his antics are many. When you are sitting quietly on the big-game stand, one will sit and watch you for a few seconds from a scrub pine, then dart around a limb and watch you from that angle, then maybe around the body of the tree for a last look before he begins again cutting on his pine burr.

CHAPTER XXVII

Fontana Village

Just a few years ago the spot where Fontana Village is now located was little more than a place on the map, with the nearest back-wilderness post office some miles away. Lying in the heart of a great mass of mountains and the heart of a renowned fishing and hunting country, it is today America's newest vacation land. When standing atop the huge dam—eastern America's tallest—and looking 'way up a lake that continues for thirty miles, or down to the gorge below, one who knew the country before all this was brought about (including the pouring of 2,800,000 cubic yards of concrete) marvels at this vast transformation which took place in the middle forties. While this great dam project was under way, people wondered if, once completed, it would be left there solitary, remote from the rest of the world. Long before it was finished, ingenious minds were convinced that this was a land of promise for fishers, campers, hikers, and vacationists. The result was Fontana Village.

The features of this remote village, so attractive to sportsmen, are its location, just below and adjoining the southwest tip of the Great Smokies; its adjacency to the huge dam that backs up a great fishing lake; its nearness to an already famous fishing and hunting country, and the various outdoor sports available in and out of the village. From this unique mountain resort the angler can cast to the virgin fishing water of Fontana, where bass, trout, and pan fish are abundant. He can go up near-by Eagle Creek, where he will find trout and smallmouth, or up Hazel Creek, the famous trout stream treated separately in another chapter. Boats are available at the public boat site just above the dam. Scenic boat trips around the lake and horseback riding along the scenic mountain trails are other favorite outdoor diversions. A sports program, including softball, tennis, and miniature golf—all this awaits the vacationist.

Guides are available for mountain-climbers and hikers, and marked trails leading from the village into the adjacent national park will direct them through magnificent settings of virgin forest and past high mountain streams where the two trouts, rainbow and speckled, are to be had in abundance. Then there is the seventy-one-mile Appalachian Trail through the Smokies, which separates North Carolina and Tennessee, and which is easily accessible by way of a by-trail leading from the village. From Deal's Gap, near the village, where the famous Appalachian Trail begins, there are nine trailside shelters about equally spaced across the higher seventy-one-mile range for the convenience of anglers, hikers, and campers. These are equipped with a fireplace and bunks. A spring is always close at hand, and camping is allowed at the shelter cabins. Individuals or parties desiring to camp in remote sections of the park not designated as camping grounds may secure permits from park rangers or wardens. They are restricted to a period of thirty days.

In the village of Fontana proper, trailer cabins and cottages of various sizes, with convenient housekeeping accommodations, are available. Located about mid-village of this frontier setting there is a retail trading center, combining a postoffice, grocery store, drug store, cafeteria, and barber shop. The village is in the heart of a famous bear country and but a short drive from the two Santeetlahs, Big and Little, where the big wild boar is king of the forest.

It is here that I plan to spend a week this summer, perhaps dur-

ing the month of June. How that week is to be spent may suggest
the ideal trip for a visiting angler at some future time. Such a trip
is different from the one- or two-day trip that means little but to
get ready and go. When it's for a week or more, the imagination
puts things together that sometimes do not fall too far short of one's
careful plans.

Two days will be devoted to the lake, casting to the shaded bays
for the two basses, and to the shoreline where the larger streams
come in, always with the probability of hooking into a large rainbow. The lures for this fishing are floating bugs, streamers, and
spinner combinations for the bays, and the two latter for near the
streams, where, in addition to bass and trout, one may hopefully
expect perhaps a musky. If the surface and near-surface lures fail to
take satisfactorily, as they sometimes do in mid-June, trolling will
be the alternative, at depths of fifteen to twenty feet or near the
depth where the fishing thermometer registers 68 to 70 degrees
Fahrenheit.

One day will be spent on lower Eagle Creek with a lure that in
previous years has been found acceptable and effective for either
rainbow or smallmouth on the lower water where these two fine
fish overlap.

To the famous Hazel Creek, where once a private fishing club
reigned supreme, as many as three days will be devoted. The boat
will be tied up near where the stream comes in fast. For this venture three classes of flies will be reserved—the always reliable spinner and woolly-bug combination, the elongated streamer that simu-
lates a frightened minnow, and on the pools and smooth stretches
twelves and fourteens in the dry fly. The first day will most likely
be spent on the lower water, where rainbow from ten to eighteen
inches may be expected. Attention will be given the expansive
Bridge Pool, where, from two center pool boulders, a twenty-

incher or better is always a probability. On the second day I'll fish on upstream, and "the glide"—still there in front of the old clubhouse site, where it was nothing to take a basket of trout without moving more than a few steps—will not be neglected. Perhaps the same day the famous Knight Pool, which holds three-pounders, will come in for attention. On the third and last day I'll go much farther up, but on the way I'll stop for a try at the little pools of Walker's Creek, mentioned in the chapter on "Little Streams," which has given me freely of its trout.

The nights in the village will probably be spent where fishermen gather. I'll listen for the familiar "What luck today?" learn what the other fellows are taking and what lures they used, and note the good hints that come along—maybe pass on one or two if there's some fisherman who isn't doing too well. Regardless of how it all materializes, these are the plans—and may they work out for me about as set forth, and for others too!

Conclusion

What has been said in this book represents many week-ends and other days when duties could be laid aside and the quiet hours devoted to recording that inborn first love—the outdoors—given to all mankind alike. With that now accomplished as best I know how, the time is appropriate to express a few final thoughts. Fishing and hunting are the two sports afield where all classes, from the country lad to men of prominence, meet on common ground, and they have given me more pleasure in a recreational sense than all else in life except my home. The enthusiasm of boyhood sprouts anew on the eve of all fishing and hunting ventures, and with the passing of each year it becomes more deeply ingrained in me.

The streams, the lakes, and the forests of these southern Appalachians are invested with a wealth of glamour that beckons the true followers of the rod and gun to follow on. The uncertainties only add charm, and whether the day's end finds us with a light creel or with shots that have gone amiss, we've listened to the rush of the falls or the music of the birds, and we retire from stream or forest knowing there'll be a return when occasion favors, perhaps even when it doesn't. Healthful exercise, mental and physical, lasting friendships, and the romance of the countryside are the priceless dividends derived from these fields of sport.

In taking my leave, I want to say this: each page has given me much pleasure as I have lived in memory some experience of the past, and, while it was written primarily for those who may be fortunate enough to visit the Great Smokies, I hope that, between these covers, there may also lie a pleasant residuum for those who may never have the opportunity to see this glorious part of our country. And now a farewell message to all whose avocation is associated with rod and gun: may the fortune of good fishing and good hunting follow you always.

Index

Abrams Creek, xxiii, 29, 63
Abrams Falls, 30, 63
Adger, Lake, 123
Alaskan Bear Committee, 144
Appalachians, xxiii, xxiv, 39, 55, 69, 85,
    122, 189
Appalachian Trail, 32, 206
Asheville, N.C., 4, 57, 60, 91, 108, 122,
    190
Azalea, xxii

Balsam Plott Hound Kennels, 184
Bass: in Lake Fontana, 80; best times
    in Lake Fontana, 81; best water
    temperature, 83
Bear, 140; numbers shot, 143;
    butchering, 155
Big Creek, 30, 31, 132
Big Black, 145
Big Santeetlah, 112
Big Santeetlah Creek, 172
Big Snowbird Creek, 112
Big Wilson Creek, 60, 61, 70
Birchfield, Nath, 154, 179
Birchfield, Sam, 154, 179
Black bear, xxiv, 139, 147–52; guides, 154
Black cherry, xxii
Black Forest, 157
Black gnat, 130
Black Rock, 182
Blasturus cupidus, 23
Bluegill, 87, 89
Bone Valley, 24, 25
Boone, Daniel, xxiv
Boone, N.C., 62, 72
Bradley Fork, 31

Brevard, N.C., 56
Bridge Pool, 207
Brook trout, xxiii, 9, 12, 19, 29, 30, 31, 33
Brown hackle, 45, 129
Brown trout, 60
Bryson City, N.C., xxiii, 41, 44, 50, 52,
    75, 81
Bryson Place, 13
Buckeye, xxii
Buffalo, 139, 158
Buffalo Creek, 71
Burke County, N.C., 70
Burnsville, N.C., 154

Cahills, 130
Calderwood Lake, 33
Caldwell County, N.C., 70
Caldwell Fork, 9
Cane River, 142
Cannibal trout, 134
Catalooch, see Cataloochee Creek
Cataloochee Creek, 3, 4, 7, 8, 9, 132,
    135
Catalpa tree, 88
Catalpa worm, 88–89
Catawba River, 70, 122
Cathey, Mark, 10, 11, 12, 13, 14, 16, 18,
    41–54, 143
Chatiage, Lake, 91–98, 100
Chattahoochee National Forest, 191
Cheoah, Lake, 32, 122
Cherokee Indian Reservation, xxiii, 182
Cherokee Indians, xxi
Cherokee Lake, 91
Cherokee National Forest, 153, 176
Chestnut, xxii

INDEX

Coachman, 129
Colorado, 8
Colorado spinner, 39
Conservation Commission of North
    Carolina, 102
Conservation Commission of Tennessee,
    102
Coot, 200–203
Crappie, 89, 121

Davidson River, 59
Deal's Gap, 206
Deep Creek, xxiii, 10, 11, 12, 13, 14, 15,
    16, 18, 41, 48, 49, 50, 130
Deer, xxiv, 185–91; hunt statistics, 189;
    location, 191
Department of Conservation and
    Development of North Carolina,
    176
Department of Conservation and
    Development of Tennessee, 176
De Soto, Hernando, xxi
Dogwood, xxii
Douglas, Lake, 118, 119
Dry fly, 15, 23, 43; uses, 3–9
Dropper worm, 22

Eagle Creek, 32, 64, 76, 205, 207
Elk, 158
Elk Creek, 71
Elk River, 62
England, xxi
Eschmeyer, Dr. R. W., 76
Esox ohioensis, 77
Euarctos americanus, 147

Fires Creek, 55
Flannery Fork, 62
Flies, 129
Fly rods, 129; lengths of, 132
Florida, 21, 88, 120
Fontana Dam, 77
Fontana Lake, 31, 32, 64, 75, 76, 77,
    78, 79, 80, 84; geography of, 75; size
    of, 75
Fontana Village, 205
Forney Creek, 31, 43, 76, 84, 132
Forney Road, 81
Forney's Channel, 82
Foote, John Taintor, 24
French Broad River, 118, 120, 121, 188
French Broad River, North Fork, 57, 58
Fungi, xxii

Gatewood, Captain R. D., 10, 13, 15,
    16, 48, 49, 50, 51, 52
Gatlinburg, Tenn., xxiii
Georgia, 91, 104, 190
Germany, 157
Ginger quill, 130
Glenville Lake, 121
Graggs Creek, 62
Grandfather Mountain, 62
Gray hackle, 11, 45, 129
Great Smokies, xxi, xxii, xxiii, xxiv, 3, 8,
    9, 11, 13, 16, 18, 19, 20, 27, 29, 30,
    40, 41, 42, 54, 55, 63, 85, 91, 100,
    102, 107, 118, 121, 133, 139, 147,
    157, 180, 205, 209
Great Smokies National Park, xxi, 27,
    75, 144, 148, 194
Green Briar Cove, 63
Greenslet, Ferris, 23

Hall, Mrs. O. C., 90
Halzworth, John, 144
Hardy's English leaders, 52
Harley, Wade Hampton, 88
Hayesville, N.C., 55, 96
Hazel Creek, xxiii, 20, 22, 23, 26, 40, 52,
    64, 76, 130, 143, 149, 206, 207
Hazel Creek Fishing Club, 20, 21, 27
Heidelberg, Germany, 181
Hemlock, xxii
Hewitt, Edward R., 51, 130
Hewitt's Gray Bivisible, 24

Hiwassee, Lake, 79, 100–106
Hiwassee River, 91, 100
Hog bear, *see* Black bear
Honest John, 144
Hooper, Newt, 154, 179
Hooper's Bald, 157

Idaho, 8
Idaho spinner, 39
India, 158
Indian Creek, 19
Iowa, 180
Ivy, xxii

James, Lake, 62, 122
Johns River, 70
Joyce Kilmer Forest, 164

Kentucky, 75
Knight, John Alden, 96
Knight Pool, 208
Kyle, N.C., 90

La Branche, George, 51
Lake bass, 78
Largemouth bass, xxiv, 76, 102, 121
Lichen, xxii
Limestone Sinks, 28
Linville, N.C., 61, 62, 70
Linville River, 61, 62, 122
Little Caney Fork, 67, 69
Little Pigeon River, xxiii, 29, 63
Little River, xxiii, 28, 29, 63
Little Santeetlah Creek, 112, 164
Little Snowbird Creek, 112
Little Tennessee River, 31, 32, 52, 63, 75, 76, 77
Little Walker's Creek, 40
Liverworts, xxii
Looking Glass Creek, 60
Lower Forney, 31, 32
Lure, Lake, 122, 123, 133
Lures, 132

Malaya, 158
Minnows, 90
Mississippi River, 147
Montana, 180
Moore, George, 157
Moore, Paul A., 169, 171
Moss, xxii
Mountain bear, *see* Black bear
Mountain laurel, xxii
Mount Mitchell, 142
Mount Mitchell Refuge, 60, 153
Murphy, N.C., 103
Muskellunge, xxiv, 77

Nantahala, Lake, 85, 90, 106, 133
Nantahala Channel, 86
Nantahala National Forest, 75, 153, 176, 190
Nantahala Range, 85
Nantahala River, 55, 75, 76, 85
National Park Service, 134
Neels Creek, 60
New River, 72
New York City, 21, 121
New York Zoological Society, 144
Nichols, Herman, 82
Night crawlers, 135
Noland Creek, 76
Norris, Lake, 91
North Carolina, xxi, xxii, 9, 20, 30, 41, 55, 56, 57, 61, 62, 64, 70, 72, 77, 90, 91, 103, 121, 133, 141, 144, 154, 158, 176, 179, 181, 207
North Carolina Bureau of News and Advertising, 95
North Carolina Division of Game, 178
North Carolina–Tennessee border, xxi
North Carolina Wildlife Federation, 164
Nymphs, 131

Oconalufty River, xxi, xxiii, 31, 64
Ohio, 102

Ohio River, 77
Oklahoma, xxi
Old Baldy, 32
Old Black, 146
Old Fighter, 6
Old Kettlefoot, 144
Old Snag, 172
Olive dun, 130
Opossum, 78
Orr, Lee, 173
Orr, Will, 171, 172, 175, 179

Panther Creek, 32, 33
Parsons Branch, 32, 33
Pisgah National Forest, 59, 60, 153, 185, 187
Plott, Enoch, 181
Plott, Jonathan, 181
Plott, Mont, 181
Plott, Vaughn, 181, 183
Plott hound, 172, 180–84
Proctor, N.C., 24
Proctor Creek, 26

Quail, xxiv
Qualla Indian Reservation, xxi
Quill Gordons, 130

Rainbow trout, xxiii, xxiv, 9, 10, 12, 14, 18, 21, 24, 25, 29, 30–33, 55, 60, 76
Raven's Fork, 31
Red maple, xxii
Red spruce, xxii
Rhododendron, xxii, 12
Rickey, Branch, 143
Robbinsville, N.C., 108, 110, 154, 179
Rock bass, 87, 89
Rocky Mountains, xxi, 72
Rough Fork, 9
Royal coachman, 8, 130
Royal preferred, 130
Ruffed grouse, xxiv, 139, 192, 196–99
Russia, 157

Russian boar, xxiv, 139, 157, 158, 162, 164, 176, 177

Sand pike, 121
Sanouke, Ed, 154, 164
Santeetlah, N.C., 179
Santeetlah, Lake, 107–17, 123, 133
Sauger, xxiv, 120, 121
Schüssehund, 181
Scotland, xxi
Sedge-colored hackle, 130
Sharpe, Bill, 95
Sherwood Forest, 153
Shooting Creek, 55
Silverbells, xxii
Slick Rock Creek, 144
Smallmouth bass, xxiii, xxiv, 102, 108, 121; size, 63; location of streams, 63, 72; record size, 78; caught with bream, 112
South Carolina, 56, 57, 191
South Mills River, 60
South Toe River, 60
Speckled trout, 31, 60
Spider fly, 130
Spinner, 131
Spinner fly, 39
Spring lizard, 90
Squirrel, 200–204
Stamey, Ralph, 187
Standing Indian Refuge, 55
State Department of Conservation and Development, 153
Stikeleather, Jim, 21, 24, 25, 52, 53
Stilwell Creek, 31
Straight Fork, 31
Stratton Bald, 172
Sugar Mountain, 144
Sumter National Forest, 191
Surface popper, 94
Swamp bear, *see* Black bear
Swan Meadow, 172

Tackle, 129–32
Tapoca, N.C., 154, 179
Tellico Mountain Plain, 169
Tellico Plains Refuge, 153
Tennessee, xxiii, 28, 29, 30, 41, 63, 91,
  118, 133, 139, 153, 158, 176, 181
Tennessee Department of Conservation,
  169
Thomason, Dr., 13, 16
Toxaway River, 56, 57
Trout: location, 30–32; in small streams,
  36–39; stream for women, 60;
  tournaments, 62; season, 133
Tuckaseigee River, 67, 81, 82
Tulip poplar, xxii
Turner Shoals, 123
TVA, 85, 91, 100, 102, 105, 121, 133
Twenty Mile Creek, 32

U.S. Forest Service, 153, 176

Virginia, 72

Walker's Creek, 26, 208
Walleyed pike, xxiv, 102
White-tailed deer, 139
White Water River, 56, 57
Wiese, George F., 70
Wilson, Adolph, 142
Wilson, Big Tom, 142
Wilson, Ewart, 142, 154
Wilson Boundary, 153
Woodcock, 195
Woolly bug, 39
Woolly worm, 15, 16, 17, 22, 131
World War I, 157

Yancey County, N.C., 142
Yellow birch, xxii